W9-CEN-180

The Dark Side
Of
Tissue Donation

The Truth Is Finally Revealed

By Christopher Truitt

Copyright 2009 by Christopher Truitt
All rights reserved under National, International and Pan-American
Copyright Conventions. No part of this publication may be reproduced,
distributed, or transmitted in any form or by any means, or stored in a
database or retrieval system, without the prior written permission of the
publisher.

ISBN: 9780557048403

2

Preface

On March 1, 1999 my wife and I found ourselves faced with the traumatic realization that our two-year-old daughter had suffered a severe brain injury and would never recover. Her body was being kept alive by a myriad of medications and machines, but her soul was already gone.

We were presented with the opportunity to donate Alyssa's organs and tissues and we offered everything we could because we felt it could help another child. Our goal was simple; to do what we could to prevent another mother and father from looking down upon their dying child knowing that nothing could be done to save him or her.

As a result of our experience with organ and tissue donation, I soon found myself changing my career by accepting a position with the very same tissue bank that had procured some of Alyssa's gifts. I was so moved by our experience, and believed in donation so strongly, that I felt I had to do everything I could to help other families understand the true scope of organ, eye and tissue donation and what an incredible thing it truly was.

Almost immediately after I was hired, though, I began seeing a side of the tissue banking industry that no donor family should ever see. I began to discover that donated gifts are reduced to dollars and cents and that profits and dividends reign supreme in the tissue reclamation industry.

For many years, tissue banks have taken advantage of the law, and also taken advantage of the donors and donor families. On one hand, the law allows tissue banks to be reimbursed for "expenses" associated with the procurement and processing of the tissue, and on the other hand, the law makes it illegal to reimburse the donor families for even a fraction of the profits the tissue banks reap from the gifts that are so selflessly given.

The public façade of tissue banks is that of caring and understanding organizations who are "stewards of the gifts," making donation possible and helping to improve and even save lives when the gifts are transplanted into the recipient.

The true nature of tissue banks, however, is much the same as every other for-profit institution: the bottom line. The manner in which they earn a profit is of less concern than whether or not they indeed do earn a profit, and how much that profit is. The truth is that the tissue banking industry earns billions of dollars each year from the generous gifts you and I both plan to give when we choose to become tissue donors.

It is important for all of us to understand what goes on behind the closed doors of tissue banks across the nation. We need to understand not just how they are taking advantage of the generosity of others, but also how they operate on a day to day basis.

Working in a tissue bank was both an incredibly wonderful and incredibly horrible experience. It was wonderful to be a part of the process of tissue donation and transplantation, yet discovering the true nature of the industry and its daily operations was nothing less than horrific for someone who had just donated his daughter's tissues.

Had I known what really goes on within the structure of the tissue banking industry, I never would have agreed to Alyssa's donation.

Tissue banks need to be exposed for what most of them are: thoughtless, uncaring and unsympathetic profit and dividend machines.

In this book I will take you through the entire donation process from start to finish. I'll explain what I see as the intricacies of the process and the inner workings of the industry, using the knowledge I gained as an industry professional.

I will expose the problems and abuses in the industry as seen through the sad eyes of a donor family member. Everything is brought out in the open; the true dollar value of a human body, the incredible profits tissue banks earn, how donors are really seen by industry executives and how donors are treated by the marketing professionals.

Organ, eye and tissue donation have always been considered as a demonstration of one of the most caring, giving acts we, as human beings, can carry out. Giving of ourselves after we die so that others may live better lives, or simply just live, epitomizes the true definition of a selfless act. The industry must never forget that simple fact and treat each donor, and each donor's gifts, with nothing less than total and complete respect.

Only when the dark side of tissue donation is exposed will the industry be forced to change the way it does business. Only then will the public demand stop the reign of profiteering tissue banks and return the industry to the altruistic endeavor it once was.

Much of the specific information contained in this book and facts used in this book were compiled from several sources including the United Network for Organ Sharing (UNOS), Organ Procurement and Transplantation Network (OPTN), and the Securities and Exchange Commission (SEC).

The information, facts, and figures were current and true, to the best of the writer's knowledge, at the time of the writing of this book. However, the writer cannot guarantee the absolute accuracy of the specific information at any point thereafter.

Credentials

Shortly after the death of his daughter in 1999, Chris Truitt began his career in organ and tissue donation by accepting a position at a tissue procurement agency in Wisconsin.   He earned his Certified Tissue Banking Specialist (CTBS) certification and designation from the American Associated of Tissue Banks (AATB) in early 2000.

Prior to, and during, his tenure at the tissue procurement agency, Chris, his family, and the family of the child that received his daughters' organs spent a great deal of time promoting organ, eye, and tissue donation. They participated in countless television news stories, provided information for print articles and spent a great deal of time talking with others about the comfort they received from thinking that their child had not lived in vain.

After spending several years at the tissue procurement agency, Chris could no longer take the mental stress and emotional strain that was created by being a donor father working within the tissue banking industry.

He left the agency in March of 2005, and decided to share the experiences and knowledge gained during the course of his tissue banking career by writing this book.

Chris's goal was, and is, to change the industry's goals and to remind the corporate tissue banks that donors and donor families make the miracle of donation possible. He also wanted to send a clear message to them that the abuse of donors and donor families must stop.

Table of Contents

omissions. Other times, more than what was consented for is taken from the donor.

Chapter 8: Next of Kin
The decision to donate or not to donate is placed squarely on the shoulders of the legal next of kin, but this person is not always the best equipped to make the decision nor to answer the questions that come with the responsibility.

Chapter 9: High Risk Behaviors
The industry has classified many high-risk behaviors, such as homosexuality and recreational drug use, as immediate donation rule-outs.

Chapter 10: The Life of a Tissue Procurement Technician
Earning a living from the death of others and their tissue donation has always presented those in the field with a set of unique emotional and mental stressors in their lives.

Chapter 11: To Err is Human
Procurement technicians are only human. Sometimes the error of just one technician can have huge ramifications for not just the donor family, but for the tissue bank and the industry as a whole.

Chapter 12: Maximizing the Gift
For as long as there have been tissue banks there have been constant struggles between maximizing a donation and taking too much.

Chapter 13: A Body's Worth
What the tissue banks won't tell you how much money a donor is worth to them.

Chapter 14: Profiteering
Greedy executives and stockholders seek to get rich from the gifts so generously donated. With annual sales measured in tens of millions and salaries of over half a million dollars for the higher-ups, tissue banking can be very lucrative for those without a conscience.

Chapter 15: Tracing the Gift
Unlike organ donation, tracking gifts and finding the final recipients is all but impossible.

Chapter 16: Both a Borrower and a Lender Be
The bottom line: if you're willing to accept a transplant you must be willing to donate yourself.

Chapter 17: Minorities and Donation
The facts are clear: minorities choose to donate far less frequently than whites, yet they make up a significant percentage of the organ transplant waiting list.

Chapter 18: Failure to Ask
Families don't automatically think about donation in their time of grief. They must be asked. Unfortunately, those charged with those duties often shrug them off, robbing families of the chance to donate.

Chapter 19: Organs & Tissues for Illegals
Why should America share such a limited, precious gift with those who are here illegally? Also, why should successful American organ and tissue donation programs share with other less successful programs?

Chapter 20: Stealing the Spirit of Donation
By profiteering, tissue banks are taking advantage of the generosity of the donors and donor families.

Chapter 21: Problems & Solutions: Introduction
An insider and donor family member's view of the problems plaguing the tissue banking industry,

Chapter 1: Alyssa – The Beginning

On March 1st of 1999 my wife and I had to make a decision that no parent should ever have to make; we had to decide whether or not to donate our two-year-old daughter's organs and tissues.

The cold, hard truth was that in the course of just 24 hours our precious Alyssa had gone from a healthy and happy two-year-old toddler to a limp and almost lifeless body lying in a Pediatric Intensive Care Unit bed with no brain activity and absolutely no hope of ever recovering.

Our "Bug" was born with congenital hydrocephalus. Everyone's brain is built to make cerebrospinal fluid (CSF). This fluid, manufactured and temporarily stored in small reservoirs in the brain, flows through an intricate pipeline that runs from the brain to, and throughout, the spinal cord, protecting the spine, its nerves, and its blood vessels.

For victims of hydrocephalus, the pipeline between the brain and the spine never develops properly, or it develops but then closes partially or even altogether. The brain, never knowing that there is a problem with the pipeline, keeps making CSF but with nowhere to go it begins to build up within the ventricles in the brain.

As the volume of fluid builds up so does the pressure on the surrounding brain tissue. If left untreated the pressure will eventually build to a high enough level that it begins to damage the cells, nerves and blood vessels that make up the brain, leading to permanent brain damage and most likely death.

Alyssa's case was discovered about two weeks before she was born, giving us enough notice to prepare for an emergency c-section and an immediate operation after her birth to relieve the pressure on her brain. Barely before she even took her first breath Alyssa was whisked away to neurosurgery. The surgeon's goal was to place a shunt (or internal plastic tube) that would route the fluid from the CSF storage areas of her brain to her stomach, slowly draining the excess fluid from her brain and relieving the deadly pressure.

It wasn't always that easy, though. Up until very recently children born with hydrocephalus were simply institutionalized. Although some were successfully shunted in time, the vast majority suffered irreparable brain damage. That coupled with the bleak outlook for those suffering from the disease caused parents to simply sign their children over to state-run institutions for people with mental and physical disabilities.

Thankfully, by the time Alyssa was born, science had triumphed over hydrocephalus and it was viewed as a treatable physical condition rather than a lifelong mental disability.

At birth Alyssa's head was literally the size of a soccer ball. Her entire body, folded up, could have fit within her head. As she developed throughout the pregnancy the CSF built up within her brain and, with the unrestrictive, flexible and moldable head of an infant, her skull and her brain were allowed to spread out as the fluid built up within. This flexibility actually saved Alyssa's life because, with no restrictions on size, her head simply continued to grow without causing a deadly build-up of pressure within.

Immediately after birth the physicians focused on managing the fragility of Alyssa's head and brain. They knew that with the right treatment and therapy, Alyssa could grow up to be a perfectly normal girl. Any misstep or mishap, though, and she could end up in a "vegetative" state for the rest of her life; completely paralyzed with essentially no real brain activity.

When Alyssa, our second daughter, was born, my wife and I were barely into our twenties. We, along with our eldest daughter, who was only two at the time, had to do a lot of growing up and do it quickly. Our entire lives changed to accommodate Alyssa's special needs and all of the physical, mental and emotional aspects of life that go hand-in-hand with having a special needs child.

Our lives quickly turned into a never ending schedule of physical, occupational and speech therapy, neurologist appointments, neurosurgery follow-ups and regular physician check-ups. We had to learn how to care for a hydrocephalic child; everything from feeding her to clothing her to having to use a special car seat, and these accommodations all made our lives, and her care, very complicated.

We did not mind the inconveniences. Alyssa was our daughter, and we simply did what needed to be done; what any parent would do. We tried to take everything in stride and care for our daughter as best we could.

We knew that over time Alyssa would need to have shunt "revisions." As her body grew, the neurosurgeons would have to replace the tubing with longer and larger tubes to accommodate Alyssa's larger body. The changes were necessary because of the increased CSF production and hopefully would stave off the inevitable clogging of the shunt over time. Every hydrocephalus patient faces the same prognosis – multiple revisions over the course of his or her life.

In Alyssa's case, though, the neurosurgeons never even had had the chance to make the first revision. Or rather, they missed the warning signs that the first revision needed to be made. On February 28th, 1999 Alyssa began showing the signs and symptoms of a shunt malfunction. The tiny plastic tube that ran between her brain and her belly was no longer allowing CSF to flow. It had become blocked.

We immediately noticed the signs and symptoms of shunt failure and took Alyssa to our local hospital early in the evening. Throughout the evening and through night the doctors ran test after test but they told us that they couldn't come up with a definitive diagnosis. We'd later learn that they had indeed diagnosed her as having a shunt malfunction but chose not to tell us. Instead, they told us she probably had the flu virus and would need to be hospitalized overnight for "observation and rehydration."

Our hospital, though, decided they didn't want Alyssa at their facility (they claimed a lack of beds as their reason) and they spent the next few hours arranging transport to another local hospital. By 3 a.m. the next morning we were finally on our way there.

As we had suspected, Alyssa's shunt was plugged and, without having a viable outlet through the shunt, the CSF began to build up within Alyssa's brain. At 4:30 that same morning the pressure became too great for Alyssa's tiny brain to handle and she fell into cardiac and respiratory arrest.

The physicians did what they could to eliminate the excess pressure immediately but the damage had already been done. Prolonged high pressure within our little girl's head had killed her. As with other similar brain injuries, the parts that control not just thoughts and feelings, but also the parts that control basic functions like heartbeat and breathing had been shut down by the pressure. Although the doctors were able to get a heartbeat back, the damage prevented any return of normal breathing. Our vibrant, friendly, outgoing and persistent daughter was being kept alive by nothing more than a ventilator and a cocktail of various medications.

She was immediately transferred back to our hospital which, in the course of just a few hours, miraculously found a bed, and placed her in the intensive care unit.

Chapter 2: The Decision

By the early afternoon of March 1st 1999 my wife and I knew in our hearts that our daughter Alyssa was already gone. Although not a single physician even bothered to take the time to talk to us or had the basic human decency to tell us what was going on, we knew that Alyssa would never wake up. We had a decision to make; a decision of which the magnitude was beyond any we could ever have imagined.

On the one hand, we could keep Alyssa alive indefinitely with machines and a mixture of medications. She would not, however, ever wake up and would never be "our Alyssa" again.

On the other hand, we could let Alyssa die in peace and choose to donate her organs to another child that still had the possibility of someday getting out of the PICU bed that held her captive. Although our daughter's life was over, we could give someone else's daughter a chance to live her life to the fullest.

We chose to save the life of another by allowing the life of our own to quietly dim and fade away. Over the years many people have asked us how we could have made such a decision. In essence, we had to allow the doctors to let our daughter die.

This was a decision that goes against every fiber of a parent's being. As parent, we would give our own lives in an instant to save the life of our children. This is a feeling so strong that only another parent could understand. It's often said that a man's instinct for his own survival is the strongest instinct in the world, but that is simply not true. To save his own child, he would gladly give up his own life, just to give his child a chance to live.

I spent hours bargaining with God. I begged him to take my life and spare Alyssa's. I promised everything I could in the hope that He would spare the life of our innocent little girl. It wasn't fair to take her – she'd done nothing wrong. I asked Him to take me instead, but my prayers went unanswered. Nothing could be done for Alyssa.

The doctors asked us for permission to perform two tests that would tell us definitively whether or not Alyssa had any brain activity of any kind, and any chance of survival, no matter how remote. The first was an apnea test in which they shut off the ventilator to see if Alyssa would breathe on her own. She did not.

The second test, as it was explained to us, actually measured the flow of blood around and through the brain. We were told that the results of that test were "not consistent with viable life".

And so it was confirmed. Our daughter was officially brain dead. On the afternoon of March 1st 1999, we not only came to grips with the fact that our precious little girl was gone forever, but we also chose to donate Alyssa's organs and tissues, hoping to save someone else from facing the decision we were now faced with. If Alyssa's gifts could save the life of another child, we decided we would give everything we could.

It was at that point that we were introduced to what we've now come to know as a "case manager;" a liaison between a donor family and the hospital or other recovery agency. It is the case manager's job to gather the necessary information so they can help the family make the difficult decisions. Medical and social histories, hospital records, blood tests – everything had to be completed and all the tests and results had to be a perfect fit for a potential recipient.

A case manger has to work not only with the donor's family but also with the procurement agency, the transplant agency, and ultimately the recipient and his or her family. It's a tough job, but one that a case manager willingly takes on.

We were taken to a quiet and dimly lit room just down the hall from Alyssa's PICU bed. The woman we spoke with was, at the time, nothing more than another blurred face asking questions and babbling medical jargon on that terrible day.

She asked the tough questions she needed answers to and helped answer our questions as well. She walked us through the general process and what we could expect to happen in the next minutes, hours and even days.

We had many concerns and she addressed each and every one. While they may seem almost ridiculous now, they were of paramount importance then. For example, we wanted to make sure that Alyssa received anesthesia during the surgery – we didn't want her to feel any pain just in case any part of her was still there somewhere. We knew she was, for all intents and purposes, already dead. Her brain was essentially lifeless, with no consciousness and no ability to feel anything but we wanted to make sure nonetheless.

Our chief concern, though, was that we did not want Alyssa to be alone. We asked the case manager if Alyssa could have her favorite stuffed animal – a miniature Winnie the Pooh – beside her during surgery so she wouldn't be alone. She told us that not only could we send Pooh with Alyssa but that she herself would be right there with Alyssa throughout the procedure.

It was then that she presented us with the second most difficult decision we have ever had to make – she asked if we wanted to hold Alyssa after the surgery before she was taken away by the funeral director. We chose to see her. No tubes, no pumps, no IVs, no ventilators – just our little girl.

While the hospital was busy working with the United Network for Organ Sharing to find a recipient, the coroner was called. He went into Alyssa's room and spoke with the doctors to confirm her death. On the way out, he looked at us and said something that burned itself into the very fabric of our being. Instead of saying "I'm sorry" or "My thoughts and prayers are with you" or anything else along those lines, he looked at us and said "Don't worry. You're still young. You can have more kids."

I was absolutely speechless. There are no words to describe the anger I felt towards that horrible man. Nothing I'd felt before, or even since, has come close to the pure rage that welled up within me and took over my body. My daughter was dead and all he could say was "you can have more kids".

Before I could react, though, we were taken back to the dimly lit room for another meeting with our case manager. They had found a recipient – a girl a year younger than Alyssa who needed a liver, pancreas and small intestine.

We gave our final consent for the donation to the case manager and were given the planned timeline. With the surgery a few hours away, we were also given time to say our last goodbyes to our precious little girl.

By this time, many of our family members and friends had made the journey to the tiny family waiting room outside the Pediatric Intensive Care Unit and each knew the exact situation. Most never spoke, but they didn't have to. Just having them there was enough to help us through our horrible ordeal. Our pastor was also there, and helped us pray for Alyssa and our family throughout the day.

Time slowed to a crawl and a seemingly endless stream of people came and went as we waited for word that Alyssa would be taken to the surgery that would end her life and be a new beginning for another little girl.

When we were told the time had come to say goodbye, our four-year-old daughter came to Alyssa's bedside with us. In all of her innocence she asked if she could sing Alyssa's favorite song to her just one more time before she was taken away. So, all of us there began to sing "The Itsy Bitsy Spider." It was a song I wished would never end. As we sang, I knew that when the song was over we would have to say goodbye, and I simply wasn't ready to do that. I couldn't bring myself to say goodbye to my precious little girl.

How can a dad say good bye to his daughter and then send her down a hall to have an operation that will kill her? How can a father send a child to her death? I knew in my mind that she was already gone. The tests had proven just that. Yet my heart just wouldn't believe it. To this very day, I ask myself what would have happened if we had said no.

As the song ended, my heart and mind slowly succumbed to reality, and after it was over I said my good-bye. With one final kiss on the lips and another on each eye I sent my little girl down the hall to die.

It was only a matter of hours, but it seemed like a lifetime that we sat in the family room waiting for news that the surgery was over and that we could hold Alyssa again. It was a surreal experience and time seemed to stand still; we still had family and friends with us but nobody said a word.

We still had our family minister there but no prayers were offered. We all simply waited in silence and solitude.

Later that night a nurse came in to take us down to Alyssa. They had set up a private recovery room just outside the operating rooms for us to share with Alyssa. As I rounded the corner in the hall and walked through the door to the room, I saw our case manager sitting in the rocking chair with Alyssa in her arms. There were tears running down her face and a painful understanding in her eyes . I knew right then that she had kept her promise and had stayed with Alyssa through it all. She made sure that Alyssa had not been alone.

From that moment on, she became a part of our lives and a part of our family. She had broken one of the cardinal rules of medicine and had allowed herself to become personally involved. By doing so she allowed herself to feel the grief and sorrow that we knew but she also made sure that our little girl had somebody there to whisper in her ear and hold her hand as the last breath left her tiny body.

I did not understand why anyone would willingly take on that sorrow. I couldn't comprehend why anyone would allow themselves to feel such heartache when they did not have to, especially for total strangers. Yet there she sat, hugging and rocking Alyssa, making sure our baby girl was not alone.

It was at that point that everything hit me all at once. The entire world came crashing down around and upon me as the realization that my daughter was dead finally broke through and took over my mind. My heart broke in two. Somehow, seeing this complete stranger rocking our daughter's lifeless body made it all real.

That night we each had the chance to rock Alyssa, to sing to her, to kiss her and to just hold her. Ironically, it was the first time in two days that we could hold her without worrying about pinching tubes, tugging on IVs or pulling off wires.

My wife was the last one to hold Alyssa. It may have been minutes or it may have been hours – I have no idea – but after a while, she quietly placed Alyssa in the crib in the recovery room, pulled the blanket up over her and simply walked away. It's a scene that has haunted me since and will continue to haunt me for as long as I live and most certainly beyond.

Chapter 3: The Recipients

In the days following Alyssa's death and donation we began asking our case worker questions about the recipient. It was important to us to find out if the transplant was a success. It was important to us to find out if Alyssa's gifts had indeed saved a life.

She had told us that she could only give us limited information; there were confidentiality and privacy issues that limited what she could say. She did tell us that the transplant was a success and that the recipient was doing better than ever before.

Undaunted by the "security and privacy issues," we began asking if we could see the recipient. We didn't need to meet, but just wanted to see the miracle with our own eyes. Over the course of several days we kept in contact with our case worker and then one incredible day it happened – she asked us if we'd like to meet the recipient and her family. Just as we had been begging to see the recipient, the recipient's family had been begging her for the chance to meet the donor family.

Nine days after Alyssa's death we were finally given the chance to meet the recipient and her family. The hospital had asked us if they could invite the media. It was so unusual for the donor and recipient families to meet that they wanted to capture the moment and use it to promote organ donation.

Another reason for the media attention was that they had picked up on the recipient's story a few months before. My wife and I had, in fact, followed their story as it was told on the local news programs. We remembered feeling so sorry for the family and hoping that they would find a donor but never could have imagined that donor would be our own Alyssa. It's odd how fate works.

We didn't care either way about the media; we were focused on meeting the little girl and her family. We had learned that she was about a year younger than Alyssa and that she had an older brother who was the same age as our eldest daughter. Her parents had brought the family down to Madison from Michigan in the hopes of finding a liver, pancreas and intestines for their baby girl.

Our first meeting was private. It was just the recipient's family and ours in a small alcove in one of the hospital's corridors. We didn't speak much at all. There were no words that could have possibly conveyed our thoughts and feelings. The bond was instant and unexplainable, and only those that have walked in our shoes could ever hope to understand it.

After an emotional greeting, the parents invited us in to meet their little girl. Here she was, only a few days after major transplant surgery, and she looked up at us with her bright eyes and smiled. It was a quirky smile; a smile that was all hers but yet was inexplicably familiar.

We learned that only days before the transplant surgery the doctors had given her only a few weeks, to possibly a few months, to live. When the family learned that a donor had become available they were elated at first, but then the realization set in that although their daughter's life may be saved another family had just lost their child.

I could never begin to understand or explain the dynamics that must play out in the recipient and recipient's family's minds. It must be a horrible fight between the incredible joy of learning your child may be pulled back from the brink of death contrasted with the incredible sorrow of knowing that your child has been saved only because another parent's child has died.

In the weeks and months that followed we became very close with the family. They would eventually sell their home in Michigan and move to within just a few miles of our house to be closer to their daughter's physicians. Our families became inseparable.

Because of the press the whole story and the donation itself generated we were the subjects of countless television and newspaper stories and features. Our story became common knowledge around the hospital and the community and our families spoke about donation to community groups, religious groups, training sessions, info sessions, symposiums, and other meetings in the private sector and medical community alike. We even gave speeches about donation at one of our Governor's State of the State addresses.

Both families had chosen to allow their pain, sorrow and joy to be displayed to the general public in the hope that our stories would help inspire others to do the same.

Chapter 4: Career Change

During this time I was working as the Building and Grounds Supervisor for a local private school. It was a great job – it was a small private school and I loved the students, the teachers, the beautiful campus and the freedom the job provided. But, despite all of this, I couldn't help but feel somewhat empty.

We had all gone through a major life-changing event and it had given me a new view of life and death and had also given me a new purpose – to promote organ donation. I enjoyed sharing our story and enjoyed answering questions. I felt that doing so helped inspire others to choose to donate. Every time I shared our story and saw the faces of the people listening I knew that I was touching their hearts. I knew that if I could share a little piece of our lives with them they might make the decision to donate as well and someone else's life might be saved.

It seems funny now, but as I was doing some routine, mind-numbing maintenance task one day a few months after everything happened, it finally hit me – I was in the wrong place. I needed to work in organ and tissue donation. In the grand scheme of things, what I was doing at that moment wasn't what I needed to be doing. I could be using my life experiences to spread the word about what an incredible thing donation; I could help other people like my family save lives.

I took a long lunch break that day and went in to the hospital where the transplant took place to see our case manager. I told her what I was thinking and asked her how I could get into the field.

It just so happened that the head of the Organ Procurement Organization (who was also the surgeon that worked on Alyssa's donation) had close ties with the local Tissue Procurement Agency. With the help of him and our case manager I found myself at the Agency's door. I had actually met the head of the Agency at a few of our speaking engagements and he gladly offered me a part-time position on the procurement team.

I immediately accepted the position. It was an opportunity to spend at least some of my time working in the field that had become such an important part of our lives and I saw it as a chance to help other donor families, like ours, through the donation process.

Now it's time to get a little specific. In the world of donation there are three main types; organs, eyes and tissues.

Organ donation is probably the most widely known and understood of the three. It encompasses the donation of "live" organs such as the heart, lungs, liver, pancreas, kidney and intestines by a donor who is alive at the time of the procurement. An organ donor is usually an otherwise healthy person that has been involved in some sort of accident that has rendered him or her brain dead with no hope of any type of recovery. The picture of an organ donor is often a young adult that is a victim of a motor vehicle accident or other traumatic injury of some sort.

Time is the most critical factor in organ donation. There is a very small window (typically just a few hours) from the time the organ is removed from the donor to the time it must be transplanted into the recipient.

Organ transplant teams can take as much time as they need to prepare for the surgery, but once the process begins time is incredibly critical. After the surgery is completed the organs must be rushed to the waiting recipient with no time to lose and no time to spare.

Tissue donation is totally separate from, and different than, organ donation. Tissue banks typically handle bones, skin, tendons, veins and heart valves. While organ donors must be living at the time of donation, tissue donors must have already passed away.

There is a substantially different timetable as well. Once a donor passes away, tissue procurement teams have between 15 and 24 hours to complete the donation process depending on individual circumstances. Once the tissues have been procured they are placed on ice in coolers where they can remain for several days before being deep frozen or processed into their final form at the tissue processing facility.

The other major difference between organ donation and tissue donation is that the criteria for a tissue donor are relatively broad whereas for organ donors the criteria can be very narrow. From the very young to the very old, almost everyone can be a tissue donor. The cause of death can be natural or traumatic and the overall health of the donor is not necessarily a big factor.

While organ donation can only take place in an operating room with numerous surgeons and support staff, many tissue procurement agencies can perform their procedures in not only operating rooms but also in county morgues and even funeral homes. Teams are often made up only of specially-trained personnel; they have no need for surgeons or physicians.

Eye donation is very similar to tissue donation in in those same ways except that instead of teams of several procurement technicians the procedure is almost always done by just one individual.

My job was that of a procurement technician on the tissue procurement teams. It's an odd job to hold. Procurement technicians must be able to drop everything at a moment's notice to rush into the office and out on a recovery case at any hour of the day or night on any day of the year.

I was on call from 5 p.m. Sunday straight through to 5 p.m. Friday. Sometimes an entire week could go by without a recovery, and at other times we could have two or three recoveries in a row on any given day.

Thankfully the staff at the school understood my need to work in organ and tissue donation and fully supported my odd schedules and hours. I'd report to work as scheduled but was given the freedom and flexibility to leave on a recovery if one came in or to come in late had I been out on a recovery the night before.

Had it not been for their generosity and understanding I could never have held my job at the Agency. However, as the months wore on and recoveries became more frequent, the strain on my full-time job at the school was becoming more and more obvious and less and less manageable. They needed someone full time who could also be on call for them and I simply couldn't do it. Two years after joining the Agency I finally had to part ways with the school.

I didn't know it at the time, but I was joining the agency in the midst of a huge organizational break-down and shake-up.

For many years the Agency was an integral part of the hospital's Organ Procurement Organization (OPO). The OPO saw the need for and value of providing the opportunity for tissue donation to those that qualified for organ donation as well as those did not.

The head of the OPO worked very closely with the tissue bank and was even on the board of directors for the agency. Many of the case workers were employed both by the OPO and the agency and often worked both jobs at the same time, coordinating both organ and tissue donation procedures for the same donor.

It was a logical partnership and it was vital to the success of both the OPO's donation and transplant program and the agency's recovery program.

Shortly before I was hired, though, a disgruntled former Agency employee fired off a few "anonymous" letters to the hospital administration, the Agency, and even the press alleging misconduct and conflict of interest because the two separate organizations were so tightly woven together.

Although most of the allegations ended up being unfounded and untrue, the damage by the negative press, negative public relations and ensuing Food and Drug Administration investigation had already been done. In the end, several OPO employees ended up resigning and the hospital demanded the resignation of the director, ending his leadership over what he had turned into one of the most successful Organ Procurement Organizations in the nation. The OPO officially terminated its relationship with the Agency and restructured itself to eliminate any future cooperation between the two.

This was the beginning of the end for the Agency.

Chapter 5: The End of the Agency

In order to understand what happened to the Agency it is important to understand the basics of tissue banking. In general, there are three parts. The first is procurement or the actual, physical "harvest" or "recovery" of the donated tissues. The second is processing during which the donated tissues are cleaned and machined into their final products., The third is the sales and marketing arm that puts the finished products into the surgeons' hands.

The Agency was a not-for-profit procurement agency. Their main purpose was to procure donated tissues and they also handled the local public relations aspect of donation and provided ongoing support for donor families. They were the "front line" of tissue donation.

Once the tissues were procured, they were sent to a processor to be turned into the final products that would be sold to surgeons. This arrangement is called "fee for service". Procurement agencies are "reimbursed" for the tissues submitted for processing. It is an arrangement designed to create the best possible public image. Donated tissues are never bought or sold. Instead, recovery agencies are "reimbursed" a set amount per tissue and these funds function as the revenue for the procurement agency.

Due to the ongoing FDA investigation and the ensuing public relations nightmare, the Agency needed more support than they could handle themselves. In what seemed like a good idea at the time, the Processor took over management of the agency to handle the new and emerging needs of the Agency during the fall-out. The Agency still kept its identity, but it officially became part of the Processor's corporate structure.

The Agency wasn't the only tissue bank being "bought out" by the Processor. In fact, several procurement agencies around the country were becoming part of the processor's corporate machine. Agencies in New York, Georgia, Alabama, Florida, Indiana, Montana, and other states would soon be under the Processor's large umbrella.

During the acquisition of the various procurement agencies, one major problem prevailed for the Processor – public opinion.

The Processor was a publicly traded company, interested in net revenues and shareholder dividends. The general public seemed to feel that any company involved with tissue donation should focus on the donors and recipient instead of the bottom line.

The management agreements that were set up allowed each individual agency to retain their company identity and not-for-profit status, although the parent company was for-profit. The Processor's first attempt at insulating the not-for-profit procurement agencies from their connection to the processor was to create a non-profit Management Group that would run the agencies.

Instead of each agency reporting directly to the Processor, each agency reported to the Group and the Group reported to the Processor. The Processor felt this would maintain the public appearance of not-for-profit agencies and insulate them from the inevitable criticism of profiteering in the tissue industry.

The public, however, saw this as the Processor's attempt to hide the truth and an attempt to cover up the fact that a for-profit company was running the individual agencies.

The Processor later dissolved the Group and for the first time the clear connection between the recovery agencies and the Processor was exposed. This was a direct attempt to dispel rumors that profiteering was indeed part of the process. They created a new Division in the Processing company which included all of the procurement agencies like the one I for which I worked.

They embraced the procurement agency connection and defended the role of a for-profit company by reasoning that profits make research and development possible and R&D results in safer and more useful products.

The bottom line, though, is that a for-profit company can have only one focus; remaining profitable by generating revenue for its stock holders. Donors and donor families were turned into nothing more than a source for raw product.

This is where the Agency was now heading. Over the years, the Processor slowly began changing the image of the Agency. What began as an independent, not-for-profit tissue procurement agency began to change into just another division of a tissue industry empire which was accountable only to its stockholders.

Chapter 6: The Donation Process

Every donation generally began, and was conducted, in the same way for most of the tissue banks and tissue procurement agencies throughout the nation. Although it most likely remains the same today, I will describe it in the past tense, speaking only from my own experience.

When a death occurred or was imminent, a member of the facility's staff called a centralized phone number for the state that was specifically set up for reporting deaths. The operators gathered basic information about the potential donor including a brief medical history and the cause of death. This was the first test for what is referred to as donor suitability; trying to determine if the donor meets certain physical, medical and social criteria required for a donation to take place.

Many donors were ruled out by this first test. Some of the medical "rule out" criteria included HIV, AIDS, hepatitis, dementia, certain types of cancer and sepsis. There were also social "rule out" criteria such as travel overseas during the UK's mad cow outbreak or the SARS outbreak, homosexual contact, having been incarcerated long term and other "high risk" behaviors.

Each of these initial criteria was designed to rule out those donors whose tissues could present a risk to the supply of clean, healthy, high-quality products.

If the potential donor passed the first test, the information was forwarded to the tissue bank for further review. In the case of the Agency, a case manager trained in determining donor suitability received the information and called the reporting person to gather even more detailed information regarding medications, transfusions, diagnoses, surgeries, lab work and blood tests.

Often the family wasn't notified of the possibility of donation until after the potential donor passed the second test. However, approaching a family about organ, eye and tissue donation can be an incredibly difficult, uneasy and uncomfortable situation no matter at what point it occurs in the process.

Many healthcare workers, funeral directors, coroners and medical examiners were afraid to approach the family, sometimes thinking that doing so would somehow cause the family more pain and grief at an already difficult time. Others disagreed with donation for their own personal reasons and choose not to bring it up at all.

The truth is that, for many families, donation was and is something they'd like to do but they either don't think that their loved one could be a donor or they simply forget to bring it up in the midst of the situation. In both cases the family has lost out on the opportunity to make something good, something positive, come out of their loved one's death.

If the family agreed to consider donation they were put in touch with an operator at a specialized call center. The specially trained operator would answer the family's questions, walk them through the donation process and then conduct the third test for donor suitability; the medical and social interview.

This interview consisted of two main parts. The first was a very personal and probing questionnaire. Questions ranging from the basic medical history of the donor to his or her sexual preferences and conduct were all a part of the questionnaire process. Speaking from my own experience, it was a difficult questionnaire for the donor family to get through, but it was a process that had to be completed to ensure the safety and quality of the tissues being procured.

The second part of the interview consisted of what the industry called Informed Consent. Although federal, state and local laws may have required different explanations and disclaimers for each agency, the consent generally included the following:

- Identification of the specific tissues that were being "requested" (those tissues that the procurement agency was interested in procuring) for donation. Each tissue or group of tissue had to be requested and consented to individually. For example, consent had to be given separately for the arms, legs, heart, veins and skin.

- Request for consent for use of the tissues in transplant, education and/or research
- Basic details of the procurement process as well as if and how it could affect final arrangements
- Request for permission to obtain the donor's medical records
- Request to obtain blood and tissue samples as needed to determine donor suitability
- An explanation that the donated tissues could be used for cosmetic purposes
- An explanation that multiple organizations, both not-for-profit and for-profit, companies would be involved in the overall process.

Informed Consent was, and is, the most important part of the donation process. It is the one and often only time a family will have full knowledge of and full control over the donation process.

Once the donor had passed this third test the donation process could begin in earnest.

It was at this point that Agency case managers spoke with the facilities, healthcare professionals, funeral directors, coroners and medical examiners involved to determine where and when the actual procurement would take place. The procurement team was called in and arrangements were made to transport them to the facility where the procurement be done.

During my time at the Agency the recovery could take place in a hospital operating room or hospital morgue, at a local county morgue, in a rural doctor's office, or even in the preparation room at the funeral home responsible for the final arrangements.

In each case the team would take with them all the tools and supplies necessary to perform the sterile tissue procurement procedures. Each procurement site was prepared with various cleaning solutions and sterile drapes, and each donor was carefully washed and prepared for the procedures.

The procedure itself usually began by the technicians making long incisions in the arms and legs and taking out the bones and tendons that the family consented to donate. In the case of cardiovascular donors, the heart and certain veins would also be removed and, depending on the family's wishes and the condition of the donor, skin may also have been procured.

When the procurement procedure was complete, all of the procured tissues were sealed in individual bags and placed in a cooler with ice for the trip to the Processor.

All of this had to be completed within 15 to 24 hours after the donor's death. Once the tissues were "on ice", though, the rush was over and the tissues had a few days to make the trip to the Processor where they would be frozen and quarantined pending final approval for use by the medical director.

Depending on the final arrangements, the donor may have been "reconstructed" by replacing the bones taken with wooden dowels or PVC pipes designed specifically for donor reconstruction and then all incisions were stitched closed. It was then up to the funeral director to continue with the appropriate final arrangements.

Even with the intensive examination of the donor's medical and social history there was still one final test to pass before the tissues could be released for processing and eventual transplant. It only happened after the procurement had taken place and the tissues had been received by the processor.

Blood samples taken from the donor had to be tested for a variety of diseases and bacteria. Cultures from the donated tissue were tested on a case-by-case basis and the donor's medical records were reviewed, also on a case-by-case basis, before the donated tissue was cleared for use. This process could take from several days to several months.

Once the tissue had been released from quarantine it began its transformation into the final product.

Only in rare cases, and with the exception of veins and heart valves, were the tissues transplanted into the recipient "as is". The vast majority of the time tissues were broken down and machined into hundreds of precision-tooled pieces including everything from bone powder and paste to tiny pins and screws or carefully crafted replacement tendons. The tissues from any given donor could yield hundreds of individual products.

After the tissues had been processed they were made available to the surgeons that would purchase them and transplant them into the recipient.

Chapter 7: True Informed Consent

The most important part of the donation process is the sharing of information between the family and the procurement agency which is called "informed consent." Families rely on the agencies to be honest, truthful and forthcoming with information regarding how the donation process will play out, including which tissues will be taken and how they will be used. Procurement agencies rely on the honesty and good will of donor families to provide not only accurate information about the donor but also the very gift itself.

There is a very fine line drawn right down the middle of informed consent. On one side there's a risk of not providing enough information for the family to make an educated decision and on the other side there is a risk of providing the family with too much specific information in a manner that would cause them to decide not to donate.

The cold, hard truth is that the procurement process is not a calm, quiet and precise surgical procedure. In many cases it can be a physically involved and exhausting process for the procurement technician. Incisions can often run the entire length of the arms and legs and entire bones must be cleared of all connective tissue. Specialized chisels and mallets are used to slice through bones which are then wrenched free from the joints that connect them and forcefully pulled from the body. It is a physically exhausting job for the procurement technician. As blood vessels are cut and internal cavities are opened during the process there is typically extensive bleeding and leaking. It is generally not quite, neat, and clean procedure.

The human body is designed to be strong and stay together to provide stability and function for the body. It is not intended to be taken apart and does not come apart without extensive efforts by the recovery teams.

However, explaining this to a grieving family while asking for consent would most certainly do more harm than good. Despite the graphic nature of the procedures, the gifts they yield will undoubtedly help others to live better, fuller lives, and may even save lives. Families may not feel that they need to know every detail of everything that goes on during the actual procedure in order to give properly informed consent as long as they are simply made aware of the basics of the procedure and are reassured that their loved one will be reconstructed afterwards

In the case of a musculoskeletal (bone and tendon) tissue recovery, it is my opinion, based on my experience, that the family needs to know their loved one will have incisions made on the arms and legs and that entire bones, along with their tendons and some muscles, will be completely removed. They also need to know that bones removed during the donation can be replaced with prosthetics and that the incisions will be closed so they can still have a viewing and funeral if they wish. The bottom line is that the procurement teams will essentially return the donor to the pre-donation condition as best they can.

Obtaining consent for skin must also be done carefully. The truth of the procedure is that oftentimes long strips are taken at what is called "full thickness". When the procedure is complete there is often nothing left at the recovery site but a thin membrane. There is often extensive bleeding and extensive leaking of body fluids at the recovery site.

However, the recovery is generally only done on the back and legs - the parts of the body that will not be visible during the viewing or funeral, and funeral directors are able to control the bleeding and leaking using a variety of techniques and products.

With this too, the family may feel that they do not need to know the harsh specifics but they do need to be made aware that skin recovery is an extensive procedure and there will be some damage done to the body. To not inform them of this fact prohibits the family from making an informed decision and giving their informed consent.

Another main part of informed consent is the potential uses of the donated tissue. Tissue processors manufacture products that can be used to heal sports injuries, repair traumatic injuries and reconstruct bodies ravaged by age and disease. These products can also be used for elective plastic surgeries, from face lifts to breast augmentations and penis enhancements. Families must be made aware of this fact.   Some prefer simply to be told that their loved one's gifts may be used for either purpose and make their decision to donate based on that knowledge and the knowledge that they will have no control over how the gifts are used. Some families will object and decline to donate while others will feel that the potential good outweighs the bad and will consent to donation.

The third and final piece of informed consent is the notification that both not-for-profit and for-profit agencies will be involved in the process. Families need to be aware that although the procurement agency may be not-for-profit, the processing company is most certainly for profit. In fact, for-profit processors make millions of dollars each year from the sale of the products created from donated tissues. Some families will consent to the donation regardless, while others will refuse to allow a total stranger to make tens of thousands of dollars from the sale of their loved one's gifts.

Chapter 8: Next of Kin

The entire organ, eye and tissue donation process relies on the actions of one person: the next of kin or NOK for short. The NOK is the person who, upon the incapacitation or death of a family member, is responsible for making all of the decisions regarding medical care, donation and final arrangements.

A common misconception is that just because someone has indicated on his or her driver's license that he or she wishes to be a donor or is carrying a signed donor identification card that that is permission enough to begin the donation process.

The truth of the matter is that virtually every procurement organization and tissue bank relies on verbal and or written permission from the NOK and few ever ask about or see the license or ID card. Although the cards may be all that is required to satisfy the legal aspect of becoming a donor, the decision almost always ends up squarely on the shoulders of the NOK.

One reason for this is that the NOK's responsibility goes above and beyond simple consent for donation. It is the NOK's responsibility not only to decide whether or not to donate, but is also their duty to go through the consent process and answer all medical and social history questions to determine donor suitability.

Although the exact sequence varies from state to state, NOK designation generally starts with the spouse and goes subsequently to the adult child, parents, adult siblings and finally legal guardian (but not necessarily in that order).

One problem with the NOK system is that the official or legal NOK is not always the person closest to the donor. Another problem is that other family members may disagree with the NOK's decisions but are legally powerless to change the decision. The Terri Schiavo case in Florida is an excellent example of the conflicts that can develop between the NOK and the family. In Terri's case, the husband wanted to remove life support and allow her to die, but the parents wanted to keep her connected to life support. The husband, as the legal NOK, had the final say.

The NOK system often breaks down when the donor is a young single adult living hundreds or thousands of miles from their parents' home. Although the parents are the legal NOK they often know little of their child's recent life and lifestyle.

Take for example a college student living in California who is involved in a fatal accident. His parents live in New York and, aside from holidays, they haven't seen their son much over the past few years. The person best able to answer the questions about his recent health and lifestyle would have been his fiancé who resides with him in California. However, she would not be legally recognized as the NOK and would therefore not be asked to give consent or answer the medical and social history questions.

It would be up to the parents not only to decide if their son should be a donor or not but also to answer difficult questions about difficult topics such as their son's sexual history and possible drug use; areas of his life which they probably know nothing about.

Some organ, eye and tissue banks are adjusting their informed consent guidelines to allow people other than the NOK to answer questions about the donor's medical and social history, but all still require consent to come directly from the NOK.

Another frequent problem with the NOK system is the inability of the coroner, medical examiner, funeral director, law enforcement or tissue banking staff to reach the NOK. Sometimes the NOK is simply not known and other times they are all but impossible to reach by phone. If the NOK cannot be reached, a donation cannot take place.

The best way to avoid any potential NOK difficulties is to make a decision now and share that decision with your entire family. It's impossible to predict who the legal NOK will be at the time of your death so the best thing to do is make sure every potential NOK is aware of your wishes.

Along those lines it is also vitally important to make your advanced directive decisions (decisions about whether or not you wish to be kept alive by "extraordinary measures") and put them in a legal document as well.

Don't burden your loved ones with these decisions. They will have enough to deal with should you be incapacitated or die. Save them from the agony of trying to make the decision for you.

Chapter 9: High Risk Behaviors

The tissue banking industry has set up certain guidelines in an effort to "weed out" unsuitable donor tissue before it is even procured. This is done for several reasons, including protecting the overall supply of disease-free tissues for transplants, protecting the procurement and processing staff, and protecting the profits of the tissue banks.

Tissue banks check the donor's information against "rule out" criteria - information about the donor's life and health that immediately rules out the possibility that that person can become a tissue donor. These are most often termed as "high risk behavior." Some of the most obvious high risk behaviors include travel outside the U.S. to the United Kingdom during the Mad Cow Disease outbreak or travel to the Orient during the SARS outbreak. Anyone falling into those two categories is assumed to have been exposed to the disease and is therefore unable to donate.

Another high risk behavior is incarceration. If the donor has been jailed for longer than a set period (typically a few weeks) he or she is automatically ineligible for donation. It's assumed that if the length of the jail term is longer than a few weeks the donor was incarcerated in a hardened penal facility and was exposed to various diseases from hepatitis to AIDS. Short stays in jail such as the few days required for certain municipal violations or minor charges don't automatically disqualify a donor.

Known recreational drug use is also a high risk behavior and grounds for an immediate rule-out. Although the exact criteria will vary, most tissue banks rule out donors known to be or even suspected of injecting drugs, assuming that dirty needles have been used. Some will still accept donors that are known to use or have used drugs such as marijuana or cocaine.

One of the biggest rule-out criteria is male homosexuality. Although some tissue banks will accept female homosexual donors, male homosexual donors are automatically assumed to have AIDS or herpes or other diseases frequently spread by sexual activity between men.

Some tissue banks will also rule out heterosexual donors that have had frequent sexual encounters with many different partners, or heterosexual donors known to have sexual contact with homosexual or bisexual partners. Again, this is done to prevent a donor with AIDS, hepatitis or any number of STDs from entering the system.

High Risk Behaviors are determined to exist by asking very specific and very detailed questions during the consent process. This is one area greatly affected by the next of kin. If the NOK is unaware of any high risk behaviors, the donor is assumed safe and the tissue bank proceeds with the recovery. Any potential diseases will hopefully (eventually) be caught by the testing performed on the tissues and blood, but by that time the entire procurement team may have been exposed to any diseases the donor carries.

Many other criteria are used to rule out potentially infected donors such as dementia of unknown origin, jaundice, cancer and various other conditions and diseases. The down side is that many of the ruled-out donors may have been perfectly healthy and may not have had the disease or condition assumed to exist from the high risk behavior.

However, the safety of the tissue supply and the procurement teams has to come first.

Chapter 10: The Life of a Procurement Technician

During my time as a tissue procurement technician no two days were ever the same. Before the Processor took over most of my co-workers and I were employed on a "per diem" basis. There were no salaries and no hourly wages. Instead, we were simply paid a set dollar amount each time we went out on a recovery. We were given a set rate of pay for a basic skin and bones recovery. If additional tissues such skin, cardiovascular, or research tissues were also procured we were given additional pay.

In a throwback to my days as a firefighter and Emergency Medical Technician, I lived life by the pager. The big difference was that instead of having only five minutes to get to the fire department when the pager went off, I had an hour to make it in to the office when a recovery was a "go."

The hours were the same. Twenty-four hours a day, five days a week. Death never takes a holiday and does not shut down for the night. The pager could go off at 3 p.m. or 3 a.m. no matter the day or weather and we had to be ready to go to work whenever the cases came in.

It was hard on my family. We could never plan on me being around for anything. I could not volunteer for my daughter's school functions and could not even be relied on to be able to watch the kids while my wife ran errands. We could not go out to eat unless we took two vehicles and I often ended up getting my meal 'to go' as the pager went off while the family stayed at the restaurant to eat.

I had to work every holiday that fell in my rotation which was especially hard on the family. I spent more than one Christmas Eve and Christmas Day out on recoveries. In fact, during the holidays the number of cases usually increased due to suicides and inclement weather.

Living by the pager was hard on all of us but we also understood the importance of the job that I and my fellow procurement technicians had to do.

Each time the pager went off the drill was the same - drop everything and head into the office. Once there, the team would be given the details of the recovery case including the donor's information, where we were going and what we would be procuring.

If the donor's location was within a few hours driving time, we'd load up the SUV or minivan with our equipment and hit the road. If the procurement was to take place farther away we'd charter a private twin-engine propeller airplane and arrange ground transportation on location to get us there in time.

There was no way to forecast when, where, or even if the next recovery case would occur. We could go weeks between cases or have two or even three back to back in one night. Sometimes we would work at one of the partner facilities locally and other times we would have to fly hundreds of miles to perform a recovery in a rural hospital or funeral home.

There was also no set time that a case took to complete. The actual on-site portion could take anywhere from a couple of hours to upwards of eight hours depending on the condition of the donor and tissues being procured.

Over the years many people asked me what life was like as a procurement technician. Some were in awe, some were appalled, and others were just morbidly fascinated. The bottom line was that my job was to sit around and wait for a potential tissue donor to die. When that happened, I'd go to work and get paid.

My job, however, was not like normal jobs. I could not simply punch out at 5 p.m., go home and forget about work until the next morning. My job followed me home and haunted my dreams.

For me, working in tissue donation was more than just a "medical" job and it involved more than just performing recoveries. Doing my job as a part of the overall donation process, I became intricately involved with helping families create something positive out of the death of their loved ones. Although they would never know who I was, what I did, or that I was even there, I helped them carry out the last (and generous) wishes of their family members through tissue donation.

I knew firsthand the value of donation. I felt the pain and sorrow of losing someone close and knew the measured joy that came with finding out that even in death a loved one could help someone else. I understood better than most the way the souls of two total strangers could become forever intertwined as a result of donation and how one person's death could save the life of another.   My personal experience made working for the Agency more than 'just a job'.

For some procurement techs, it was, and is, "just a job." They were there because of the money and that was all they cared about. With the opportunity to earn a salary or hourly wage for working in the office in addition to the $300 to $500 for each recovery, the money is most certainly there. Many procurement techs can make from about $50,000 to over $100,000 per year.

In speaking to and working with other procurement techs at the Agency and across the country it was clear who was there just for the money. They fought about who was in line for the next case and often tried their best to work the on-call system to ensure they would receive as many cases as possible. This poisoned the recovery end of the business with a dollars and cents attitude instead of maintaining reverence and respect for the donors and donor families.

When I first started out as a procurement tech I found myself becoming somewhat emotionally involved in each and every case. I couldn't help but be reminded of the loss that the family was feeling. When I went to perform the recoveries I was not simply performing a medical procedure. I was helping someone help others even through death.

Over the years, though, this emotional involvement began taking its toll on me and I had no choice but to try to distance myself from the donor and donor family. Dealing with death day in and day out at first makes you appreciate life. But, unless you find a way to deal with the negative effects, it can also lead to depression and that was the road I was heading down.

I had to learn to look at each case as a "day's work" and operating rooms, morgues and funeral homes as nothing more than my "office." I could not let myself become emotionally involved in every case and had to learn to treat the donation as strictly a medical procedure, focusing on the end product – the medical appliances that would be transplanted into recipients. Donors had to be nothing more than pieces of anatomy and the procurement had to be nothing more than a procedure that was performed on an anatomical "thing."

This is not to say that I became hardened and emotionally uninvolved. I could never allow myself to become so detached that I turned into one of the money seekers. I was always acutely aware that each donor was a person and that he or she left behind family who would miss them.

There were also the really hard cases; the cases that I could not detach myself from and the cases that haunt me to this day.

Some of the most haunting cases involved young donors. There is a natural progression to life. We are born, grow up, grow old and then pass away. Most of our donors were elderly or had succumbed to long battles with illnesses and disabilities. Although these donors would be missed, their death was still within the natural order of things. It was expected and it was understood.

When a child dies, though, it simply isn't natural. Children are supposed to bury their parents; not the other way around.

Normal recoveries involving bones, tendons, skin, heart valves and veins took place on donors as young as 14 and as old as 99. Every once in a while we would get called out to recover tissues from a teenager. Those cases were always more difficult physically, mentally, and emotionally. Some were victims of accidents and others were simply victims of their own minds. It was hard to justify their deaths and hard to come to grips with the fact that such a young life would never be given the opportunity to blossom and mature into what it was meant to be. In an odd twist of fate, the young and strong tissues from these donors were often the most desperately needed.

The agency also performed heart valve recoveries on children, toddlers and even infants. I was, thankfully, never asked to perform such a recovery. I doubt I could have made done it, having had to bury my own young child. Even hearing about these cases broke my heart because I knew exactly what the parents were going through.

Along with that, though, I was incredibly relieved that the families chose to donate. Just as I knew the pain and sorrow firsthand, I also knew the healing that donation creates. It allows families to create something positive from something so horribly painful.

Some of the other cases that haunted me did so due solely to their circumstances. Some were suicides, others were murder victims and yet others were simply victims of a horrible twist of fate and fluke accidents.

One case in particular involved a wife who, on her husband's birthday, was hoping to surprise her husband by working one of his many odd jobs for the day and then take him out to dinner with the money she would earn from that job. Instead, she had a freak accident on the job, was killed, and instead of treating her husband to a birthday dinner, her husband had to make her final arrangements.

Another recovery took place on a couple of teenage friends that were involved in a horrible vehicle accident. There were two sets of parents mourning the loss of their children that night.

There were also recoveries performed on child abusers, wife beaters, murderers and other people that can only be described as the scum of the earth. It was hard to allow them to be a part of something as wonderful as donation. However, in those cases, we simply focused on the family and how what we did helped them cope with the death of their loved one.

I often wondered how the recipients would feel, or if they would even want to know, what kind of person the donor was.

For every haunting case like those, though, there were dozens of others that were easy to cope with and understand. The great-grandpa that passed away at 99, the husband and wife that died together in a car accident after 40 years of marriage, the disabled person that was finally free of his earthly prison – all of those cases helped remind me of why my work was so valuable.

Even the "good" cases, though, began taking their toll on my mind and my soul. Earning a living from the death of others is a hard thing to do, and one of the aspects of my job and performance that most disturbed me was our means of coping with the stress and emotions of doing just that.

As a donor family member, prior to becoming a procurement technician, I had convinced myself that the donation process must certainly be a quiet and somber procedure. I forced myself to believe that each member of the team understood the value of the life of the donor and felt that each would treat the donor with nothing less than the utmost respect and consideration. I was sure all those involved would be saddened by the death and understand the grief the entire family was feeling.

As a procurement technician, though, this would be an almost impossible task. When a person spends each day working in the aftermath of death and destruction, he has to distance himself from the overwhelming emotional involvement. He must treat each case as a surgical procedure on human anatomy. If a procurement technician were to treat each donor as the family wished, he would simply go insane from the grief and sorrow.

One of the hardest things about being a procurement technician is how immune to the job we had to become. People working together in a restaurant joke and laugh with each other. People working in an office share e-mails and funny stories. People working in service jobs often find humor in the little things and laugh about them. Humor is a way of passing time and coping with the work day; without humor, fun, and laughter, spending time at your job becomes unbearable work. Working in the procurement industry was, in that respect, no different than any other job. We needed to laugh too. We often joked about our jobs and what we did. We found humor in the little things and ironies surrounding recoveries. We found ourselves deeply involved in only the anatomy of the donor and the procedure of the recovery, and distanced ourselves as much as possible from the emotion. We had to treat each case as "another day at the office."

To this day I find myself wrestling with how I had to act in order to survive as a procurement technician versus how I hoped my daughter's procurement team would have acted. I would not have wanted my daughter's recovery procedure to be conducted as I myself conducted recoveries, but I could not handle each recovery as I would have wanted my daughters' handled or I would have gone insane. To think about someone laughing and joking while procuring my daughters organs and tissues chills me to the bone – yet that is exactly what I found myself having to do just to maintain my sanity.

The bottom line, though, is that I loved what I did for a living – not what I did on a daily basis, but rather the part I played in helping families with donation.

Chapter 11: To Err is Human

The ultimate responsibility for carrying out the final wishes of a tissue donor and the donor's family lies squarely on the shoulders of the procurement technician.

It is up to the technician to verify that all the necessary pieces are in place and that procedures are followed to ensure that each gift consented for is recovered.

There are volumes of information that procurement teams must take into account for each recovery and base their decisions on; information that may or may not be 100% accurate and information that may or may not be verifiable.

Each recovery begins with a review of some sort of brief synopsis of the case information. It provides basic details about the donor, the tissues to be recovered, the location of the recovery, the pertinent coroner or medical examiner's name and whether or not there will be an autopsy. Also to be reviewed are whether or not there are any restrictions placed on what can be recovered and the name and contact information for the funeral director that will handle the donor's final arrangements.

Added to this is a copy of the actual consent of the next of kin. It is the responsibility of each team member to review the consent form to ensure that only approved tissues are recovered.

However, when teams are on their second or third back-to-back case with little or even no sleep, mistakes can be made. I have heard of times when teams not only recovered but also shipped tissues that were not on the consent list. For example, arm bones were taken when the family specifically denied consent for the arms.

These errors were eventually caught and damage control went into full swing. Because of these cases, changes were made in procurement operations across the nation so that teams had to verify the consent at several points during the procedure and ultimately verify that only consented tissue was recovered.

Another key task was to verify the identity of the donor. This may seem like basic common sense but there have been instances of procurement teams mistakenly performing recoveries on totally different bodies.

At times, verifying the donor's identity may actually be quite difficult. The donor's identity is often not considered verified unless the body has an identification bracelet or tag attached to it by a coroner or medical staff. Oftentimes, though, the donor was rushed to the hospital as he or she was dying and in the confusion of trying to save his or her life the hospital never got around to giving their patient an ID bracelet.

After death is pronounced the body is often wheeled directly to the morgue and never receives an ID bracelet. Although the donor may be the only body in the morgue, recovery teams still require some form of identification. At this point they may call one of the facility staff members who worked on the patient to verify ID or they may rely on the morgue staff to print up and attach the identification tags.

This is an even bigger problem when the recovery is performed at funeral homes where there may be more than one body in the room. The funeral director is often relied upon to positively identify the donor.

Once the donor's identity has been confirmed the next step in the procurement process can take place.

In certain cases, procurement teams are also required to obtain copies of the donor's recent medical records and review them for information pertinent to the suitability of the donor.

This information may include everything from recent blood test results to diagnoses of certain diseases and conditions to the volume and type of fluids and medications given during the last hours of life.

It is up to the team to then determine if the donor is suitable for procurement. If key things such as sepsis or dementia of unknown origin are discovered the donor will be deferred and the procurement will not take place.

The donor must also be closely examined physically to ensure that certain conditions that are indicators of health problems or high risk behavior are not present. For example, needle marks between the fingers and toes indicate possible drug use and the donor should not be recovered. Certain types of discolorations and sores may indicate different diseases that would automatically render a donor's tissue unusable.

Once in a while, in reviewing the information, the team may make a mistake and decline (or defer) procurement for a donor that was actually suitable. In those cases someone must explain to the family why the gifts were not procured. For a family that agonized over the decision to donate and was subjected to the emotionally charged and mentally draining consent process, this notification may come as a devastating blow.

The actual procedure itself can also fall victim to the errors of the procurement staff. If the donor is not properly prepared and cleaned certain bacteria may contaminate the tissue and render it unusable.

Likewise, if any tissue is inadvertently put in contact with an unclean surface it may become contaminated and cannot be used for transplantation.

The quality of the procured tissue itself is subject to the skills and abilities of the procurement team. An errant slice in a tendon or nick in a bone can significantly reduce the tissue's potential uses, and if a vein is sliced or punctured it can easily be ruined.

Once the procedure is complete there are still more possibilities for human error. Mislabeling the tissues can lead to a mandatory discard. Misprinting information in the recovery paperwork submitted with the tissue can lead to total denial of all of the tissue by the processor.

The way in which the tissues are packaged and shipped can have also grave effects on the tissues usability. If too little ice is used in the transport coolers, the tissues may warm to a critical level. If the individual bags within the coolers are not sealed properly, the contents may spill out and everything in the cooler could become unsuitable for donation.

Even if the procurement is performed flawlessly and the tissues are packaged and shipped properly and reach the processing center in perfect condition the tissue may still be subject to human error.

If a blood test or tissue culture is not performed to exacting standards the test results may indicate the presence of bacteria or other organisms that render the tissue unusable as was the case with my own daughter's heart valves.

In addition to donating her whole organs, we also chose to donate her heart valves. We found out several years after the recovery that her heart valves were declined due to a positive Hepatitis test even though we know that she did not have Hepatitis. It was most likely the result of a false positive, mishandling of the tissues, or a flaw in the test taking procedure.

The bottom line is that the ultimate responsibility of ensuring that each gift is used and the donor's final wishes are carried out comes down to a human's ability to do his or her job and is affected by many external factors.

Although these factors are measured by the procurement agencies as tissues and dollars lost, they are measured by the donor families as the loss of an opportunity for something good to come from their loved one's death. It is a chance they will never get back. It is a chance that, if blown by stupid human error, is gone forever.

If a restaurant cook has a bad day, someone's dinner is burned. If an accountant has a bad day, a decimal is put in the wrong place. If a procurement technician has a bad day, though, an entire family's hopes and dreams to make something positive come out of their loved one's death are ripped apart. Likewise, the recipient eagerly waiting for those tissues loses his or her chance for the skin graft for their burn, the bone for the hip replacement, or even the vein for their cardiac bypass.

Chapter 12: Maximizing the Gift

A popular phrase among tissue banks is "maximizing the gift." It is a phrase intended to mean that procurement teams should make the most out of each donation, procuring as much of the consented tissues as possible to make the final gift as meaningful as possible.

However, in the world of profits and stockholders, "maximizing the gift" means taking as much donated tissue as possible so as to maximize the profits from each and every donor.

The difference between the two is subtle but the ramifications are huge. Instead of managing the procurement agency with focus set squarely on the donors and donor family dynamics, "maximizing the gift" means running the agency focused on the bottom line.

For tissue banks, procurement is the beginning of it all. It's the part of the process that provides the raw materials for the rest of the process to function. In the eyes of the corporate tissue banking world, obtaining donated tissues is thought of in virtually the same was as a pizza restaurant thinks of buying the meats and vegetables it will use to make the pizzas. It's a crude comparison but a very accurate and truthful one.

The focus of for-profit tissue bank companies is quite simple: sell the final products to make lots of money, pay the shareholders their dividends and watch stock prices soar. Their goal is to get the most raw materials for the least amount of money, process it as inexpensively as possible and sell it for the highest price possible, hence their version of "maximizing the gift."

Tissue banks are in quite an interesting situation. Instead of having to buy the raw materials, they essentially get them for nothing, relying upon and often taking advantage of the generosity of donors and donor families to provide the raw materials. Their main goal is to take as much raw material from each donor as possible.

One of the problems of for-profit tissue banks is tempering the "get it all" mentality with the knowledge that they have not been given the go-ahead to ravage the donor and to take every last scrap of raw material, but instead have been given the raw material as a gift. They oftentimes forget that it is indeed a gift and that they are beholden to the giver.

Although the tissue banks may measure the donated tissue in square centimeters, tensile strength, ounces and grams, the donor families measure the gift in memories, love, joy, and sorrow. It's not just a bone or a tendon; it is part of their loved one and that fact must never be forgotten.

When procuring donated tissue it is vitally important to understand that the donor's family took part in the informed consent process. They spoke with a tissue banking professional about their gifts. They were given explanations about how the procedures would be done, which tissues would be taken, how they would be used, and finally in what condition the donor would be returned to them.

Those working with the families are inclined not to bring up details about the specifics of the procedure in an effort to save the family from having to see their loved one and the donation process in the eyes of the unrelated and uncaring corporate tissue bank mentality. The technicians performing the procurement, however, must approach the process from the corporate mentality of 'maximizing the gift'. Details are inevitably lost in the process.

An excellent example of this is a technique called "full thickness skin procurement." In a normal skin recovery a surgical instrument called a dermatome is used. Part electric razor and part scalpel, the dermatome shaves the top few layers of skin off the donor's body in swaths a few inches wide. The skin can be so thin that it's virtually transparent or as thick as a substantial fraction of an inch.

Skin is typically recovered from the legs and back – areas that will be covered up by clothing during the viewing and funeral. A full thickness graft which was being tested for a skin processing center during my time at the Agency and it was being procured free-hand from the chest.

In an exacting procedure, the procurement tech cut a 12 to 24 inch square in the middle of the chest. Then, using nothing more than a scalpel, the tech carved the skin square free from the underlying tissue. At the end of the procedure a 12 to 24 inch square hole was left in the chest with nothing left but a thin membrane keeping the contents of the chest cavity in.

According to the Agency and the Processor, this fell within the scope of the consent for skin under the guise of "maximizing the gift." Their mentality is that the family consented for skin so they could procure as much as possible.

However I, as a donor dad myself, saw the procedure as incredibly barbaric. My own personal opinion of donation is simply this: anything can be taken as long as the donor's body can be returned to basically the same condition in which it was found if that is the family's wishes. Procured bones should be replaced with prosthetics, incisions should be stitched closed, skin recoveries should still leave a few layers on the body and nothing should be procured from areas of the body that will be visible during the viewing, visitation or funeral. Although many tissues are being taken, the donor should still remain as "whole" as possible in appearance.

I reasoned that since the free-hand skin recovery procedure disfigured the donor to a point that it could not be "repaired" the family needed to know about the procedure and give specific consent. Fellow procurement technicians across the US and even many of the funeral directors that received the experimental donors felt the same way and the procedure was ultimately discontinued – but only after countless recoveries were performed using the technique.

Another horrifying aspect of "maximizing the gift" occurs when the donor will be directly cremated without a viewing of any kind. Direct cremations are often thought of as a "free for all" by the corporate tissue banking world. Since the donor will not be seen after the procedure, the rules don't apply and virtually anything can be procured to "maximize the gift."

This was especially the case when tissues were procured for research. Agencies typically partnerd with several research firms to provide tissues for scientific research projects ranging from cancer to AIDS to aging, and even to be used by students for educational purposes. Samples were regularly taken from all of the body's organs and systems, including the liver, intestines, prostate, kidney, lymphatic system, veins and more.

Occasionally, though, researchers requested items such an eyelid, entire ear, entire foot and other similar specimens. Again under the guise of "maximizing the gift," these tissues would be procured and sent off to the researchers when the donor was to be cremated without a viewing.

Although the families officially consented for research, taking these specimens abused that consent. Again, "maximizing the gift" was slanted to benefit the tissue bank without regard to its true meaning for the donor family.

Some families would have no problem donating such tissues for transplant or to promote scientific research, study and education. Many would gladly give whatever can be used for any purpose.

Other families though, such as mine, would never consent to such procedures because of their barbarity. Even though the donor is dead and gone, mutilating the body is simply not acceptable.

In any case it should be up to the family to decide. Any procedures that remove parts of the body that cannot be replaced by artificial means need to have special consent. Any procedures that disfigure the body in a way that cannot be closed or repaired, such as the free-hand skin recovery, need special consent.

Maximizing the gift is one of the many problems inherent to the involvement of for-profit companies in the tissue banking world. Tissue banks must serve one and only one master – the donors and their families. For-profit companies, by their very nature and definition, serve many masters - from the board of directors to the shareholders or stockholders. In the capital-focused corporate world, profits almost always trump all else.

Chapter 13: A Body's Worth

One of the most taboo aspects of tissue donation is the actual dollar value of a donor's gifts. It's a topic that no tissue bank is willing to discuss, yet it is a topic that is vitally important to the industry as a whole, beginning with the donor and ending with the recipient

Before continuing, it is important to understand some of the key factors that play a major part in how profits are termed, made and handled with respect to tissue donation.

In 1983 a Virginia company headed by H. Barry Jacobs announced plans to allow donors to sell their kidneys for up to $10,000. Recipients would buy the kidney at the set price and also pay a $2000 to $5000 broker fee to Jacobs.

The medical community, general public and congress were so alarmed by this that in 1984 Congress passed the National Organ Transplant Act (NOTA), which made it illegal "for any person to knowingly acquire, receive, or otherwise transfer any human organ for valuable consideration for use in human transplantation if the transfer affects interstate commerce." The law classifies an "organ" as "the human (including fetal) kidney, liver, heart, lung, pancreas, bone marrow, cornea, eye, bone, and skin or any subpart thereof and any other human organ (or any subpart thereof, including that derived from a fetus) specified by the Secretary of Health and Human Services by regulation." The law goes on to clarify that valuable consideration "does *not* include the reasonable payments associated with the removal, transportation, implantation, processing, preservation, quality control, and storage of a human organ."

Congress created the law to prevent the commercialization of the organ and tissue industries and the potential abuses that come with that commercialization. For example, the poor and destitute might be inclined to sell their own organs and tissues, or those of a family member, for the sole purpose of being paid. Or, someone might be killed just to obtain organs and tissues for a sale.

There are two blatant loopholes in the law that tissue banks regularly exploit to make their imillions in the billion dollar tissue industry. The first capitalizes on the fact that non-transplant tissues can be bought and sold, and the second capitalizes on the "reasonable fees" allowed under the law.

The definition of transplant is a common sense term - the taking of a body part from one person and inserting it into another person. NOTA clearly states that tissues which are transplanted cannot be bought or sold. It makes no mention, however, of non-transplant use such as education or research. Tissue banks can literally put a price tag on any part of the human body and sell it as long as that part will not be transplanted into another human.

Many tissue banks see the potential profits in providing tissue for research and include it as a revenue generator in their procurement programs. When a family consents to the use of their loved one's tissue for research and education, they are unknowingly giving their consent for a tissue bank to take parts from their loved one's body and sell them for a profit to a research or education organization.

During the course of regular tissue procurement, additional research specimens are taken and forwarded to an appropriate research company. In turn, the research companies pay the agencies a set price for each tissue it provides. Because the tissues are not used for transplant it is perfectly legal for the agencies to sell the tissues and make a profit from that sale.

The second loophole is the most widely abused: reasonable fees. NOTA allows tissue banks to charge what it calls reasonable fees for the "...removal, transportation, implantation, processing, preservation, quality control, and storage of a human organ." The law does not define reasonable fees, and there is virtually no regulation, so abuse is rampant industry wide. The reasonable fees loop-hole is where the tissue banks make the majority of their millions. They may charge as much as they'd like for the end product, building in overstated expenses for the procurement, transportation, preservation, quality control, storage, and processing. A typical screw made of bone and manufactured from donated tissue, for example, may sell for anywhere from a few dollars to a few thousand dollars, depending on how much the tissue bank charges for their "reasonable fees".

Because tissue processing agencies cannot buy tissues outright from the procurement agency, a "fee for service" arrangement is set up. As each donated tissue is sent to the processing agency, if it meets all suitability criteria, the processing agency "reimburses" the procurement agency for "reasonable fees" associated with the recovery. In short, the procurement agency sells the tissue to the processing center.

The actual dollar amount procurement agencies are reimbursed is one of the most closely guarded secrets of the tissue industry. Only a select few employees know the true figures. Most of those that work in the tissue industry will never know the true value of a body.

Based on the information I was able to glean over the years, I can estimate that a processor typically reimburses over $10,000 per donor and, based on the prices of the finished items sold to surgeons, the final product from one donor could be valued at upwards of $100,000. I could not find a single person in the company willing to discuss the actual figures, and was never able to confirm my estimates.

It's easy to understand the true scope of the finances involved in the industry when considering that each tissue bank will procure hundreds of donors each year and each processing agency will see thousands of donors pass through their facilities on an annual basis.

Despite the billions of dollars passing through tissue banks each year, donor families receive nothing. Tissue banks hide behind the law that prohibits the sale of tissues for transplant, neglecting to inform the families that tissues may be sold for profit, for education, and for research. They take advantage of the "reasonable fees" payable to the tissue banks for all of the activities surrounding tissue donation, processing and transplant.

Since 1984 many individual states have tried finding ways to give at least some small financial token back to the donor families who so graciously offer their loved ones' tissues.

Kansas, for example, unsuccessfully tried to pass a bill that would have provided tax credits for donations of blood and body parts. The Kansas Attorney General struck the bill down as illegal, saying that it would have provided the "valuable consideration" that was banned by NOTA.

Other states have tried to find ways to allow for the donor family to receive some form of payment for their deceased loved one's gifts. Pennsylvania unsuccessfully tried to set up a reimbursement program that would have paid $300 directly to the involved funeral directors to offset the costs of the final expenses for a donor.

Connecticut tried to pass a bill that worked within the framework of "reasonable fees" by providing a tax credit of up to $10,000 for living donors. The credit would have applied to transportation, lodging and lost wages directly related to the donation. Wisconsin and Georgia passed virtually identical bills.

Although these bills do much to reimburse living donors for their expenses, they fail to address deceased organ and tissue donors. Furthermore, the money being reimbursed comes from the taxpayers and not from the organ and tissue organizations that directly profit from the donations.

Here again the tissue banks are allowed to continue to reap their huge profits from the generous donations of individuals. Congress needs to address the loopholes and find some way to either eliminate profits altogether in the tissue industry or find a way to pay the families their fair share.

Chapter 14: Profiteering

Under the guise of non-profit or not-for-profit tax classifications and hiding behind NOTA, tissue banks are trying to perpetuate the myth that nobody is getting rich from organ and tissue donations.

The emotion behind this charged topic is simple: no donor family wants to think that some company executive is driving around in a Jaguar purchased with an exorbitant salary earned from the sale of donated organs and tissues. Unfortunately, though, that's exactly what is happening.

In reviewing the Securities and Exchange Commission filings and stockholder reports from one prominent tissue processing company, the true magnitude of the money being earned by this one company alone is very obvious.

In 2003 this company listed net revenues at $75.5 million, and in 2004 that number climbed to $92.7 million. In 2003 executive compensation packages added up to over $1.4 million dollars, with the CEO alone earning over half a million dollars.

In 2005, available bonuses for these executives ranged from $250,000 for the CEO to $90,000 for the Vice-Presidents, and totaled $710,000 together. This is in addition to the four percent raise that was approved for each executive's salary.

There is no shortage of money in the corporate tissue banking world and each and every dime is earned, in essence and in fact, by selling tissues donated in an act of good will by the donor and donor family. The CEO of just one company out of many earned over half a million dollars in a year directly from what so many people donate freely and generously.

One of the frequently-used defenses for the presence of profiteering in the tissue banking industry is that profits are necessary to make research and development (R&D) possible. Companies argue that without the backing of profits and stockholders, R&D would be all but impossible.

One company touts that their firm was able to research and develop a system which effectively sterilizes the final bone and soft tissue products before they're released for use in transplant surgery. This sterilization eliminates the risk of passing any potentially harmful biological material from the donor to the recipient.

Their patented invention and process does address a critical need for "safe" tissue. In fact, a lawsuit filed against another tissue bank claimed that harmful biological material from the donor was not only passed on to the recipient via the tissue but eventually caused the recipient's death.

In my opinion as a donor dad, former employee of the industry and former stockholder, profiteering is about more than just securing R&D funding. Every publicly-traded company is ultimately owned and operated by the stockholders and stockholders are ultimately interested in only one thing: profits. They want to see increases in stock prices and increases in dividends. The majority could care less about the true scope of the company they own stock in.

New advances in tissue banking can often be driven by profits, not morals and ethics. By having the newest and greatest products or processes the company secures its place as an industry leader, and being a leader usually translates into increased revenues and an increase in both stock prices and dividends.

Because the end result of better and safer products is achieved, tissue banks can easily say that the advances in tissue banking are driven by the need for those better and safer products and profits are simply a means to achieve those advances or even a byproduct of the advances themselves.

For-profit companies do not corner the market on profiteering. Not-for-profit companies share equal responsibility in taking advantage of the gifts. This is evident not just in the tissue banking world but in organ donation and transplantation as well.

A common misconception is that because an organization is non-profit or not-for-profit the company is run on a conservative budget. Nothing could be farther from the truth. Executives of not-for-profit tissue banks can earn multi-hundreds of thousands of dollars a year.

The bottom line is that the recipients of donated organs and tissues are paying thousands upon thousands of dollars for the product or products needed for their surgeries, and those costs are fueling a huge money-making machine.

Tracing the money trail from the beginning, it's easy to see how so many people are paid, and some paid very well, using money made from a generous donation.

Beginning with the donation, the facility at which the donation takes place is often paid a fee for use of their facility. The tissue bank staff performing the procurement takes their cut as do the procurement organizations' administration. The funeral directors responsible for embalming and final preparations for the donor often receive a set fee as well, meant to offset the increased costs of preparing a donor's body.

Once the organs and tissues have been procured they must be transported. Organs must often travel by jet, ambulance or police to reach their destination, racking up thousands of dollars of transportation expenses along the way. Tissues are often sent to the processing center by way of commercial shipping companies and can result in hundreds of dollars in transportation expenses.

Once the tissues reach the processing facility they are stored, tested, and machined into the final product. The processing agency earns their healthy profits when the end products are sold to the hospitals, and to surgeons that will do the actual transplant surgery. In the meantime, though, the sales staff and their company take their piece of the pie.

The actual transplant procedure is where the journeys of organs and tissues meet again. The surgeons, staff, hospital and administration all charge their fees not just for the transplanted tissues but the procedure itself.

At the end of the process is the recipient, whose insurance company foots the final bill.

Between donation and transplantation, literally hundreds of people take a cut of the money generated by the donor family's generous gift.

The picture presented by tissue banks and organ procurement organizations often hides all the action between donation and transplantation and rarely discloses all of the hands that grab their cut of the profits made from the final sale of the family's donation.

Donor families see nothing but the rosy picture of their loved one's organs and tissues being used to better the lives, or even save the lives, of the recipients. It is a noble, charitable and altruistic picture. Nobody suspects that behind the scenes so many people are earning such a healthy living off the gifts. If the general public were to truly understand the sheer vastness and magnitude of the profiteering within the industry, the industry would be forced to change.

But, until then, tissue banks will continue to pay millions of dollars in salaries and benefits, all created from the sale of donated tissue and, hiding behind the law, will never share even one cent of those profits with the people that made it all possible.

Chapter 15: Tracing the Gift

One of the questions most frequently asked by donor families is how the donated tissue will be used. Many follow up that question by asking if they can find out who, either generally or specifically, received their loved one's tissues.

When organs are transplanted it's very easy to keep track of who receives the organs. Immediately after a family decides to donate, a specific recipient is found for each available organ.

Depending on the policies of the facilities involved, donor families may be given very general information about the recipient and the recipient can even be given general information about the donor. In rare circumstances, such as my own, the recipient and donor family may be allowed to contact each other.

Tissue donation is a totally different situation, and donor families are rarely given information about the specific tissues transplanted or the recipients of the tissues, due to the fact that so many different products are created from donor tissue. Also, many months or even up to a year or more can pass before the final products are used in transplant.

The tissues from one donor alone can be machined into virtually any combination of over 70 different types of surgical products, and each donor can potentially yield hundreds of individual items. The individual items can be sold nationwide over the course of many months.

As each individual tissue is brought into processing it is weighed, measured and sometimes even x-rayed to determine which product types, and how many individual pieces it can yield, in a manner that maximizes the gift. In other words, the processing techs try to find the best way to use every square inch of the donated tissue by turning it into a variety of different products.

Once the product has been fully processed and the tissue has passed all of the necessary tests, it is made available for sale to surgeons, and could be shipped anywhere within the US to be used in surgery.

Once the finished products have been processed, they are treated more like medical appliances than donated tissue. Instead of using metal or plastic plates, pins, dowels, screws or wedges, many surgeons simply opt to use allograft (human donated tissue) pieces instead.

Because of the sheer volume of allografts created, the thousands of possible purchasers, and the sheer number of recipients, it is virtually impossible for any donor family to track the usage of their loved one's gifts.

Some tissues such as veins, heart valves and skin are a little easier to trace, but even in these situations the donor families are rarely given any information about the recipients.

One of the sad truths about tissue donation is that the donor family is rarely able to learn anything about how the gifts are used or who they may have helped. Their loved one's gifts are reduced to bar coded medical appliances sold nationwide or even internationally and used in hundreds of different procedures from the life saving to the life-enhancing to the purely cosmetic.

It is the possibility of use in cosmetic surgery that many families object to, and often the reason that many families choose not to donate. Donated skin, for example, may be used to help a burn victim heal, or it may just as easily be used in breast or penis augmentation. The problem is that the donor family has no say over how the donated tissue will be used. Once it is donated it becomes the property of the tissue bank and they may do with it whatever they choose.

Another objection that many donor families have is knowing that there is no control over where the product will end up. Donated organs are made available first to potential donors in the local area through the local organ donation program. If the organs cannot be matched to a local recipient they are then made available to a larger area. To put it simply, the gift remains local and may help the donor family's family, friend or neighbor.

Once donated tissue is released for sale, it can end up anywhere nationwide and sometimes even worldwide. There is no control. It may end up at the local hospital to be used to reconstruct a young driver's face after a horrible accident or it may end in a Beverly Hills plastic surgeon's office and be used for elective cosmetic surgery.

Chapter 16: Both a Borrower and Lender Be

No matter where I go and no matter who I talk to about what I did for a living I often hear "oh I could never donate..." My next question is always, "Would you accept a donated organ or donated tissue if your life depended on it?" The answer is almost always "yes."

People generally have a variety of reasons as to why they do not want to donate. Some reasons are honest, truthful, educated and well founded and others are petty and flippant, but whatever the case the end result is the same: a person that is unwilling to donate is almost always more than willing to receive.

Some people, myself included, will never agree to donate tissue because of the despicable and, in my opinion, criminal, handling of the donors, donor tissue and profits. The thought of some corporate executive vacationing in the beachside condo he bought with the money he made from the incredible and selfless generosity of tissue donors and donor families makes me ill.

Before I knew the full truth about tissue donation I donated my Alyssa's heart valves to the tissue bank. Thankfully, the tissue bank was unable to use them and I do not have to live with the knowledge that someone got rich from my daughter's death at least as far as her tissues are concerned. I will never put myself or my family in that position again.

I will never consent to tissue donation for the very reasons covered in this book. I will, however, be first in line to donate my eyes and organs, and will do so without any reservations.

It is important to understand that organ and eye donation is different from tissue donation, and that we each have a choice when the time to donate comes.

Organ donation covers an immediate need with an immediate solution. There is a critical shortage of organs and thousands of people die each year waiting for one. Tissues, on the other hand, are often in great supply. There is rarely a shortage of processed tissue and even when there is, artificial devices are usually available in their stead. In fact, many tissue procurement agencies are often told to stop procuring specific tissues because of a surplus in the system.

When agreeing to donate, the donor family has lots of choices. Depending on the actual physical circumstances of their loved one's death they may be able to donate eyes, organs and/or tissues including skin, bone, tendon, heart valves and veins. Families can pick and choose what to donate. My family, for example, will agree to donate my organs and eyes but decline tissues. Others may choose to donate organs, heart valves and veins.

With all of these choices it is easy for someone to find a way to donate despite objections to certain situations and specific details. The bottom line is that the donor family has complete control over what is donated.

I have long thought that before receiving a transplant of any kind, whether it is a cornea, blood, skin, organs, bone, veins or any other type of transplant, the recipient should first have to sign an organ, eye or tissue donor card. It doesn't matter what type of transplant the person receives or which type of donation he or she chooses, but every recipient should have to agree to donate something themselves. Those that are unwilling to donate should be denied the transplant they are hoping to receive or, at the very least, placed at the bottom of the transplant waiting list.

Why should someone receive a transplant when he or she has no intention of ever returning the favor?

This is one of the biggest problems with organ and tissue donation nationwide. In the year this book was written there were more than 85,000 people on the waiting list for organs and, of those, around 6,000 died waiting. In the time it takes you to read this book cover to cover, about 30 will have passed away.

It is estimated that there are around 12,000 eligible organ donors each year nationwide. Of the eligible donors, roughly 54 percent of the families consent, some 39 percent decline and about 16 percent are never asked.

The sad truth is that the number of available organs will never meet the demand. An argument against organ donation that I often hear is that one donor won't do any good anyway, with so many people waiting.

My response to that is to share an old story I learned about an old man, a young boy and starfish.

While walking the beach, an old man saw someone in the distance leaning down, picking something up and throwing it into the sea.

As he came closer, he saw thousands of starfish that the tide had thrown onto the beach. Unable to return to the ocean during low tide, the starfish were dying. He saw a young boy picking up the starfish one by one and throwing them back into the ocean.

After watching the seemingly futile effort, the old man said to the boy "There must be thousands of starfish on this beach. It would be impossible for you to save all of them. There are simply too many. You can't possibly make a difference so why even try?"

The young boy smiled as he picked up another starfish and tossed it back into the ocean. "It made a difference to that one," he replied.

The same holds true for organ donation. The truth is that tens of thousands of people desperately need a life-saving transplant and thousands will die waiting for one. Although one person can't save them all, almost every person can save at least one.

My daughter Alyssa's gifts did not make even a small dent in the number of people that die each year waiting for a transplant but they did make a difference in the life of one young girl and her family, and that is what donation is all about.

Chapter 17: Minorities and Donation

During the five or so years I worked in tissue donation I participated in hundreds of procurements and was familiar with hundreds more. One of the things I noticed over the years was that the vast majority of tissue donors where white Americans. There seemed to be a fairly even split between the sexes and a fair representation of all age groups but in general minority donors were few and far between.

The number of minority donors I personally saw could almost be counted on one hand. There were a few African American donors, a couple of Hispanic donors, one American Indian and a couple of donors of mixed ethnicity. When compared to the hundreds of Caucasian donors, the racial disparity becomes blatantly obvious.

There are no solid statistics for minority tissue donation and transplantation but the statistics for organ donation and transplant seem to be fairly representative of the tissue side as well.

Figures taken from the 2003 and 2004 data available through the United Network for Organ Sharing (UNOS) and the Organ Procurement and Transplantation Network (OPTN) show that only Caucasians, African Americans and Hispanics are becoming organ donors in percentages that closely match population percentages. Another interesting point is that virtually all ethnicities other than Caucasian have a higher percentage of members waiting for transplants than the percentage of the US population that their group makes up.

Minorities should be especially concerned about organ and tissue donation because, according to UNOS and OPTN data, minorities are more likely to need organs than their Caucasian counterparts. For example, Native Americans are four times more likely than Caucasians to suffer from diabetes. African Americans, Asians, Pacific Islanders and Hispanics are three times more likely to suffer from kidney disease. All will need kidney transplants.

Reasons for the donation disparity range from not fully understanding organ and tissue donation to an unwillingness to donate because whites (or other ethnicities) might receive the gifts instead of the donor's own ethnic group.

Many polls have been conducted over the years to try to glean any solid information as to why minorities, who make up about half of the organ waiting list, are so apt not to donate. A 1993 Gallup Poll showed that only 69% of African Americans support organ donation compared to 87% of Caucasians and 75% of Hispanics.

The poll showed that minorities were more likely to believe that brain death is reversible, more likely to place higher importance on the body being whole at burial and generally not seeing that there was (and is) a shortage of organs.

Many of these misconceptions correlate directly with the level and quality of education received. Other polls have shown that those with a better education are more willing to donate than those without, indicating that lesser educated groups do not understand the need for donation and the overall process.

This also ties in directly to a general mistrust of the medical community. Many feel that if a person is an organ and tissue donor that the doctors will chose to let him or her die solely to obtain the organs for transplant. This distrust is more prevalent within minority groups and especially African Americans. The truth, though, is that no person is ever allowed to die simply because he or she is an organ donor. Organ and tissue donation is only brought up after all efforts to revive the person have failed or the prognosis is hopeless.

Many organizations around the country are trying to address the ethnic disparity in donation. The Minority Organ Donation Education Program, the Minority Organ Tissue Transplant Education Program and virtually every Organ Procurement Organization and tissue bank have their own methods to promote donation among minorities.

In my opinion, this all boils back down to one simple premise: if you are not willing to donate organs, eyes or tissues then you should not be allowed to receive them, no matter what race or ethnicity you are.

Chapter 18: Failure to Ask

The process of organ and tissue donation begins when a nurse, doctor, corner, medical examiner, funeral director or other person designated as a "requestor"' takes the initiative to ask a family if they've considered organ, eye or tissue donation.

Unfortunately, many of those charged with the duty of being a requestor choose not to mention donation and although true statistics will never be known, this situation is far too common.

There are many reasons that would-be requestors choose not to mention donation. Some equate asking about donation to begging for spare parts. Some are afraid of upsetting an already emotionally charged situation, and some simply do not know how to approach a family about donation.

Another dynamic is added to an already difficult situation when the donor or donor family does not speak English. If the requestor is to communicate with the family regarding donation he or she must work through a translator who, more likely than not, has no experience with donation and can easily yet inadvertently sway a family one way or the other.

Yet another dynamic is added when the requestor and family are not of the same race or ethnicity. Certain boundaries are perceived to exist between ethnicities and one goes right down the middle of organ and tissue donation.

There are two possible scenarios for requesting. The first is that the family is willing, and often eager, to participate. The second is that the family is horrified by the thought and declines. There seems to be little middle ground between the two. There is usually no way to tell ahead of time which way the family will go.

A major misconception regarding requesting is that requestors must "sell" donation to the families. Many unfortunately see the job of a requestor as trying to talk the family into donating. This simply is not the case. No family can be "sold" on donation and it is not the requestor's job to try. Instead, many families will have specific questions and rely on the answers given by the requestor to help them decide.

Throughout the years I have spoken with many families about donation. Some chose to donate, some chose not to donate, and a disturbingly high percentage were never asked about donation and now regret that they weren't able to make the choice.

One common thread among all donor families is that they feel donation has helped them cope with the death of their loved one. Seeing something as positive as donation come from something as horrible as death helps ease the pain of their loss in at least a small way.

By knowing that some part of the donor will live on and help others, his or her death doesn't seem so stark and cold.

Many families will never be given this chance, though, because they will never be asked about donating their loved one's organs, eyes or tissues.

Many organ, eye and tissue banks address this problem by sponsoring, or even coordinating and running, requestor training programs. During the course of these programs, potential requestors learn some of the basics of donation, from suitability criteria to common family questions to basic procedural information.

Those who attend the classes are given the tools they'll need to be able to speak with families at the difficult time of death, and to do so in a caring, compassionate and educational manner.

While I was at the Agency, I shared my story and ran 'question and answer' sessions at many of these classes. I felt it was important for requestors to hear things from a donor family perspective and to be able to ask the hard questions about what a donor family does or doesn't think and more importantly does or doesn't want to know.

If more people would take the time to understand donation themselves before trying to talk to potential donor families, no family will ever have to regret not being given the opportunity to at least consider donation.

If every potential donor family was approached in the right way by the right people, organ, eye and tissue donation rates would increase significantly, and more lives would be touched, or even saved, by donation.

Chapter 19: Organs and Tissues for Illegals

One of the most incredible things about the United States is that, generally speaking, we take care of our citizens and, whether good or bad, anyone else that finds themselves within our borders legally or illegally.

In 2003 there was a huge firestorm when a story broke that a young Mexican girl smuggled into the US received not one, but two heart/lung transplants. The first set of organs ended up being the wrong blood type due to doctor error so they immediately found and transplanted a second set. The girl died anyway.

It is a tragic story, and one that, as a father, breaks my heart. Here are these poor parents who knew that their daughter would never have received the life-saving transplant she so desperately needed because they lived in Mexico. They gathered together as much money as they could and snuck into the U.S. to give their daughter at least a fighting chance at getting the transplant. What parent wouldn't do the same?

For this one example of someone in dire need of a life saving transplant, though, I can give you 86,000 others and the vast majority of those are legal United States citizens.

At the heart of the issue is whether or not organs and tissues should be made available to illegal aliens. According to the United Network for Organ Sharing (UNOS), available transplants for non-resident aliens (legal or illegal) must be limited to five percent of the total number of transplants for that organ. In other words, if 100 hearts are transplanted at any given transplant facility only five can go to aliens.

This percentage is an overall figure. It does not mean that the first five percent must go to aliens, nor the last five percent, or that five percent absolutely must go to aliens at all. It simply caps the availability of any given organ for aliens at five percent of the total transplanted. Aliens are allowed on the waiting list and their need for an organ is rated the same as everyone else's. Only when the transplant rate for their particular organ reaches the five percent level for aliens is citizenship taken into account, and only then does it become a deciding factor. If the little Mexican girl had been illegal alien recipient number six, she would have been denied the transplant. However; how does one determine the numbers and at what point do doctors actually start looking at citizenship? It is a great idea but that, I'm afraid, simply isn't practical given the limitations of our current organ transplant system.

The reason that I'm against illegal aliens receiving US organs is the same reason that I feel organs should not be shared with other transplant regions within the US itself: if "outsiders" can come and get our organs, where is the motivation for the "outsiders" to develop their own organ and tissue donation programs in their own areas?

Allowing this to happen simply compounds the problem. If no organs or tissues are available in my area it would behoove me to develop a program to increase the rate of donation so organs become available. If I can travel a few thousand miles to receive my organ instead, I would be less likely to go through the difficult work of promoting organ and tissue donation and more likely to simply head to another region where my chances of receiving and organ are greater.

Those in Wisconsin are fortunate, with about 30 donors per million residents per year. The national average is 21 donors per million residents and some states, such as West Virginia, fall as low as zero donors.

Common sense would say that with so many organs needed, every single transplant region and every single state should start improving their organ and tissue donation programs. If every state could have donation rates on a par with Wisconsin, a significant percentage of those waiting for transplants would actually have the chance to receive them.

The same holds true for other countries. If there is such a dire need for organs in Mexico or any other country for that matter, those needing the organs and their friends and families should start pushing hard to improve the donation programs in their countries.

The answer is not to go to those that have organs and steal them away. The answer is to create availability in your own area.

There are numerous successful donation programs throughout the US, and every single one of those programs would be more than willing to help the not-so-successful programs turn their operations around. There is absolutely no reason for any state to do as poorly as West Virginia and there is every reason for every state to do as well as Wisconsin.

Getting back to the problem of organs and tissues being given to illegal aliens, and the above notwithstanding, I personally would allow it on only one condition: that the recipient, and recipient's immediate family, must register as organ, eye or tissue donors in the US.

If you are willing to receive a transplant you must also be willing to donate.

Chapter 20: Stealing the Spirit of Donation

I have said much in this book about the shortcomings of the tissue banking industry as a whole as well as the shortcomings of individual companies. I have touched on the greediness of everyone involved, from the procurement technicians to the corporate big-wigs, and have decried their lust and zeal for nothing but profit.

I have showcased the various ways that the industry is taking advantage of the goodness of donors and donor families, and have illustrated the extent to which they are victimizing them.

A few years ago I was attending a ceremony put together to honor the memories of several past donors procured by the Agency. During the ceremony each family was given the opportunity to stand up in front of the group and share a story or simply say a few words about their loved ones.

About halfway through the ceremony, an elderly woman approached the podium and began speaking about her husband who, at the age of 90, had passed away and was able to be a tissue donor. I recognized the name. I was one of the procurement technicians that had procured her husband's gifts and I remembered the case vividly because of the uniqueness of the case – her husband's age.

The woman shared a few stories about the kind and generous nature of her husband. I then saw a heart-breaking change in her face. A look of great pain and sorrow replaced the smile as she talked about how hard it was to become old and to realize that both the body and the mind are becoming weaker. Both she and her husband felt sadness and guilt because they had faded from strong, contributing members of their community to what they felt they had become - useless people waiting to die.

Tears welled in her eyes and her lips began to quiver as she described how wonderful it was to find out that her husband was not as useless as they both had felt; that even at their age, in their health and their condition, her husband could give his tissues and help better or even save another life. They were not useless. Their lives had meaning and even their death could have a purpose.

She thanked God for tissue banking, thanked the agency for allowing her husband to be a donor and for showing her in life and him in death that every person can make incredible contributions to the world no matter what their age.

This is one of the most incredible parts of tissue donation, that virtually anyone can be a donor regardless of his or her situation. It gives everyone hope that even in death we can still be useful and still follow what makes us so human in the first place – our incredible desire, and even need, to help others.

Tissue banks have learned to capitalize on this. In their quest for profits they have failed to realize what an impact donation truly has on the donors and donor families. Then, when a donor family member such as me learns of the true nature of tissue donation, we are crushed. Anger, rage, grief, regret, sadness – it all comes to the surface when a donor family member learns that the CEO of the tissue bank that they just donated their loved one's tissues to earns over half a million dollars a year by turning around and selling that tissue for use in elective plastic surgery.

It reduces an incredible gift to nothing more than a profit machine.

Some tissue banks such try to present themselves as "donor focused" by creating donor family support programs and ceremonies. Many have staff that do nothing but find ways to promote donation and honor the donors and their families.

While working for the agency I was invited to share my story, the story about Alyssa, with the staff at the Processor's location. I got up in front of hundreds of employees and poured my heart out, talking about how wonderful donation is and how much it means to not just the recipients, but the donor families as well.

As I left the building, I looked over at the executive parking spaces and saw a row of cars that I would never be able to afford to own. It was at that moment that everything clicked into place in my mind and I finally realized how horribly perverse the tissue banking industry truly is.

Chapter 21: Problems and Solutions Part One – Introduction

In the preface of this book I said that it was not my intention to dissuade anyone from becoming an organ, eye or tissue donor, but rather to expose the problems with the system in the hope that they would be addressed and ultimately fixed.

Tissue donation is, and will always be, an incredible experience for the donor families. It will always be vitally important to the health and life of the recipients. It will also always be at the center of heated debates about every aspect of the process from start to finish.

Historically, tissue banks have tried to hide the nature of their involvement in the donation, processing and transplantation process from the public. Every once in a while, though, a story is written or news segment is run that brings to the forefront the ugly truth that tissue banks are often in it just for the money.

Each and every time this happens, donation rates, not only for tissues but organs and eyes as well, plummet. Donation is a very emotionally and socially-charged issue, and it is human nature to shy away from such issues anytime controversy is present.

The key to the long-term survival and viability of tissue banking is for each and every organization and company to always be 100 percent forthright and 100 percent honest. It is much easier to be proactive than reactive. When reaction is the only course of action, people will die from a lack of the lifesaving transplants that have all but disappeared already due to negative public perception.

I personally struggled with this very fact when deciding whether or not to write this book. I know all too well that many who read these pages will be so turned off by the abuses in the industry that they'll opt not to donate at all.

In the past I've ridiculed the writers of news articles and producers of news segments that portray donation in an unfavorable light because of the simple fact that negative publicity has a negative effect on donation.

However, I chose to write this book hoping that enough people will see tissue banks for what they are and push hard enough for change that the industry will finally be forced to deal with the issues that are always whispered about but rarely dealt with out in the open.

I am not one to simply cry foul and point out all of the problems. As an industry insider and a donor family member, I am in a unique position to be able to understand all sides of the issue and to try to find meaningful solutions that will benefit everyone involved, from the donors to the tissue banks to the recipients.

It is with this in mind that I present the final three chapters of this book: solutions for the problems that plague the tissue banking industry. The problems with the industry, as I see them, can be grouped into three categories: Informed Consent, Maximizing the Gift, and Profits and each of the following chapters will show how easily each can be corrected.

Chapter 22: Problems and Solutions Part Two
– Informed Consent

I mentioned in Chapter Seven that most states require certain information regarding the donation and donation process to be specifically presented to the donor family for their approval.

There has always been a delicate balancing act between providing enough information for the family to give informed consent and overloading them with too many details that could ultimately force them to deny consent.

Any person working in an industry related to death and dying knows all too well that there is a fine line between what people need to know and what people want to know. Death is, and always will be, an untouchable, taboo subject in our society.

For true informed consent to occur, families should really know how each of the procedures will be performed, what tissues will be taken, how they will be used, who will be involved in the process, and what the end result of the procurement procedure, or the donor's post-procurement condition, will be.

For example, according to the true definition of "informed consent," families should know that procuring skin will leave relatively deep swaths of missing dermis several inches wide all over the donors back and legs. Families should also know that when bones are taken, prosthetics will be installed in their place to help maintain appearance.

However, many families would not want to know the specifics. They'd instead simply like to know that there will be some external evidence of recovery, but that by and large the donor will be returned to as close to their original condition as possible.

The problem with using this approach to informed consent is, as I mentioned earlier in the book, the tissue banks taking advantage of it and assuming that because the family consented they can recover whatever they like, and that they don't necessarily have to return the body to some semblance of its original condition.

What then is the answer? Should those taking informed consent provide specific and often gory details or should the tissue banks abide by the general rule of thumb that they can only procure what can be replaced with prostheses or otherwise cause a body to be made whole again?

The answer is simple. Most families do not want to hear gory details about how the tissue bank will cut up and part out their loved one. Instead, tissue banks need to simply offer to provide detailed information. For those families that do not want the information, tissue banks must operate by the "make it whole again" rule.

If the tissue bank seeks to recover tissues that cannot be replaced or covered up (made whole again), such as in the example of free-hand skin recovery or an ear taken for research, the tissue bank must obtain specific consent for that procedure.

Using the example of the free-hand skin recovery, the family should be told that the tissue bank would like to recover a large section of skin from the donor's chest. They should be told the procurement team will be unable to reconstruct or replace the tissue taken and that there will be a visible lack of skin in the procurement area, but that the removal site will not be visible once the donor is prepared for viewing. The family should also be told that the reason the procurement team would like to take the large skin graft is because there is a huge need for large grafts in non-cosmetic reconstructive surgery.

Another aspect of informed consent that must be properly conveyed to the family is the fact that a for-profit company will ultimately sell their loved one's donated tissues for a profit.

I have heard many stories of donor families finding out long after the donation has taken place that a for-profit company earned money from the sale of their loved one's gifts. The family become irate, and justifiably so, because they did not remember anyone mentioning the for-profit aspect to them.

Sometimes, during the course of informed consent, the family is notified. However, at that time, it simply does not sink in. I know firsthand that when you're speaking to someone about the donation of your loved one's eyes, organs and tissues, that due to their emotional state at the time, much of the conversation will never be remembered.

That is why it is vitally important to inform the family of the for-profit aspect in several different ways at several different times during the consent process. For example, when asking for consent for skin, the family should be told that the skin procured will eventually end up at a for-profit skin bank where it will be processed and sold at a profit for both medically necessary and cosmetic applications. When consent is asked for bones, the family should be told that the bones procured will eventually end up at a for-profit tissue processing center where they will be processed and sold for a profit for use in both medically necessary and cosmetic applications.

By repeating the message that the tissues will be sold for a profit and used in both medically necessary and cosmetic applications, the family will have ample time to hear, digest and ultimately understand that for-profit entities will be making money from their loved one's gifts.

Another often overlooked aspect of informed consent is informing the family that the procurement may not happen at all or that all of the procured tissues may not be usable. It's important for the family to know up front that due to their loved one's physical and medical condition the procurement team may not procure all tissue consented for, and that not all tissues procured may be usable.

In the event of a motorcycle accident, for example, the procurement team may not be able to recover skin due to "road rash." Another example is automobile accidents in which bones are broken and rendered unusable by the tissue bank. In both these examples, the family should have been told that the possibility existed that the tissues might not be suitable for procurement or transplant.

This must also be followed up on by contacting the family after the procurement and informing them which, if any, tissues were unable to be procured. I personally was never told that my daughter's heart valves were unusable, due to the positive blood tests, until after almost five years of inquiring and digging through information and medical records. This should never happen. Families need to be told not only what will be used but what can't be used.

When, and only when, these issues are corrected will we be able to claim true informed consent.

Chapter 23: Problems and Solutions Part Three – Maximizing the Gift

Tissue banks and their procurement teams must reprogram themselves to think of "Maximizing the Gift" in terms of the donor families.

The corporate definition of procuring every square inch possible must be replaced with the donor family definition of making the most out of what is donated.

This is where the "made whole again" rule is key. If procuring something from the donor will leave the donor disfigured, then that particular item should not be procured unless specifically consented for. Leaving the donor disfigured should be defined as being unable to replace procured tissue with prosthetics or not being able to hide the procurement site with sutures or within, or under, a sutured incision.

Donors that will be cremated without a viewing present an incredible opportunity for horrible abuse of "maximizing the gift," especially when research has been consented for.

It was on one of these donors that I recall an entire foot being taken and sent to a research facility. I've also heard of entire ears, eyelids, fingers, toes, and more, being procured and sent in for research. The general mentality is that if nobody will see the body, anything goes.

True, the family consented for donation but no reasonable person would expect that consent to include permission to mutilate the donor's body in such a manner.

There are certainly families who would have no problem with such tissues being taken or having the body disfigured. However, I know that the vast majority of families would be sickened to find out that such things were done to their loved one without their knowledge or permission.

The problem is that there are many levels of personnel employed by tissue banks, from the procurement teams to the CEO. Each step up the corporate ladder further removes the employee from the donor and donor family perspective and closer to the net income aspect. By the time the CEO level is reached, donors are thought of as nothing more than a smorgasbord of raw materials. With that thinking, the

CEO instructs the procurement teams to "maximize the gift" by procuring every square inch of available tissue.

There is no easy external solution for this problem. Repairing it, unfortunately, rests solely on the corporate mentality within the tissue bank.

The best way to approach it is to again use the "made whole again" rule. If the procurement teams cannot make the donor whole again, then special consent must be given by the family for the procedure that would disfigure the donor. Only if that specific consent is received should the procurement teams continue.

Another easy way to handle this problem is from the bottom up. If the procurement teams would simply stop and ask themselves the "what if?" What if that was my mom or dad, sister or brother, son or daughter – how would I want that person to be handled?" The second step in this solution is not to think like a procurement technician, but rather like a lay person not privy to the inside world of donation. Only then can a proper decision be made.

Chapter 24: Problems and Solutions Part Four – Profits

Profits and profiteering are the single most critical issues surrounding tissue donation. The heart of the matter is twofold. First, someone is turning a profit from your loved one's generous gifts and second, not a cent of that profit will be shared with the donor family.

The National Organ Transplant Act (NOTA) has given tissue banks not only the legal license to do just that, but also legal protection from having to share the profits with the donor families. NOTA, in essence, makes it illegal for donor families to receive any sort of reimbursement for their loved one's gifts while allowing some CEO to get fat from the profits.

There are two things that need to happen. First, NOTA must be repealed or amended to allow organs and tissues to be sold for profit. If lawmakers are afraid that this will lead to rampant abuse, then certain laws could be put in place. The for-profit world need to be acknowledged and managed, not hidden and allowed to take advantage of donors.

Some of the most altruistic families will indeed be incensed by the notion of receiving payment for their loved one's gifts. My solution to that is to use the money to set up a scholarship, or donate it to a local charity, as yet one more way that the donor is able to help others even through death. I personally would seed a scholarship fund, so that not only would my daughter have helped through organ and tissue donation, but also continue to help for years to come through the scholarship.

At the very least the funds could be used to offset the skyrocketing costs of final arrangements and burial or even used to pay down any outstanding medical expenses incurred by the donor.

True, there may very well be some who try to abuse the system, but it is the same for just about everything else in life. To deny the donor families and guard against the profiteering tissue banks is a much bigger problem than a handful of potential abuses.

As the system stands today, the entire tissue banking industry is run off the backs of donors and donor families. The entire industry earns exorbitant profits because the law not only permits it but also requires tissue banks not to share the profits. We give the tissue banks both the raw material and the license to profit from it and this must change.

Chapter 25: Conclusion

Throughout the pages of this book I have brought to light many of the abuses routinely conducted by the tissue banking industry. I have pointed out how they occur, why they occur, and what must be done to stop them. I have done all this by giving personal examples and opinions as well as cold, hard facts learned from my experience in the industry and as a donor dad.

Some have undoubtedly found my honesty appalling and barbaric, and perhaps even consider it sensationalism, while others have realized they have finally received answers to some of the burning questions surrounding tissue donation.

No matter what your opinion, the fact remains that this information is now "out there," printed in black and white, and must be dealt with.

As I have stated previously, I know full well that some who read this book will be so appalled by what they read that they will choose not to donate tissue. I myself fall into this group. After witnessing the things I did during my career in tissue donation, I have chosen not to be a tissue donor.

The crime, though, is letting it stop there. I chose to write this book not to thrash the industry, but try to force it to rise to a level of honesty and integrity that has previously not been attained.

Do not simply put this book back on the shelf and let it gather dust. Take action. Call your lawmakers, call your newspapers, call your television stations, and call the tissue banks themselves to demand action. Demand that they acknowledge the problems in the industry and demand that they fix them. Demand that they treat donors and donor families with the respect they deserve and demand that the systemic abuses stop.

If the solutions I have presented here are taken to heart, tissue donation could once again be returned to the incredibly selfless and single most valuable act any human being can make. To give part of oneself so that others may live, or live better, will forever be an ultimate display of our compassion and our humanity.

Made in the USA
Middletown, DE
09 December 2019

80302379R00073